GOOD GOLF GUIDE

TO SCOTLAND

To my father
who took me to the
small courses
a long time ago.

GOOD GOLF GUIDE

TO SCOTLAND

by **David Hamilton**
with a foreword by SEAN CONNERY

PELICAN PUBLISHING COMPANY
GRETNA 1998

First published in Scotland in 1982
By Canongate Publishing Limited

First Pelican printing, June 1984
Second printing, January 1998

Library of Congress Cataloging in Publication Data

Hamilton, David, 1939-
  The good golf guide to Scotland.

  Reprint. Originally published: Edinburgh: Canongate,
1982.
  Includes index.
  1. Golf—Scotland. 2. Golf—Scotland—Directories.
I. Title.
[GV984.H36 1984]   796.352'06'8411   84-3141
ISBN: 0-88289-446-3

Manufactured in the United States of America

Published by Pelican Publishing Company, Inc.
1101 Monroe Street, Gretna, Louisiana 70053

Designed by Gordon Watson

Contents

Acknowledgements

I am glad to thank many golfers and club secretaries in Scotland who have answered my questions and who received me hospitably on my travels around the land in search of good golf.

I am grateful also to Mrs Grace Anderson and Mrs Isobel Gray, who cheerfully typed the manuscipt.

Lastly, my father, the Rev J. Hay Hamilton carefully read and commented on the text.

Foreword
by Sean Connery

To be asked to write a foreword for a golf book such as David Hamilton's splendid "GOOD GOLF GUIDE" provokes in one a chain reaction of emotional memories and souvenirs that any third-rate psychiatrist would have a field day with. On the backward journey with oneself the "trip" encounters blackouts, brainstorms, touches of madness, orgasmic pleasures, fantasy behaviour — that under normal circumstances would be totally unacceptable to anyone in their right mind — whatever that means! The terrible beauty is that in the brotherhood of golf (feminists please excuse the term) we are all the same — certifiable: the mutterings to no one in particular, with a whine in the voice that loving parents would not permit in their own children; the numbing disbelief at the lack of justice; glazed eyes, somehow, hissing "What luck!" through clenched lips and teeth; not to mention the callisthenics on the course in search of that elusive swing.

The great Jack Nicklaus summed things up neatly during a charity match on the Old Course at St. Andrews where he and I were playing against Ben Crenshaw and Glen Campbell. I asked him what he considered to be the most important factor to overcome in the game of golf. His reply, "It is an unfair game."

To me it is more than a game — as Michael Murphy so aptly captures in his "GOLF IN THE KINGDOM". I toast all the Jekylls and Hydes I have encountered in its pursuit.

The amount of literature on golf is enormous and will obviously continue. At the time of writing, Jack Nicklaus is revealing in *Golf Digest* how he is changing his swing, having broken all the records over 20 years (not only for first place but also for second). My own shelves have more than their fair share of Dobereiner and McCormack & Alliss.

The beauty of Hamilton's book is the abundance of information, whether seated by the fire on a winter's night with a glass of the best, playing an immaculate tee to green over

Scotland's best, or planning an entire golfing holiday. It has the know-how to handle the sometimes delicate approaches necessary to gain access to the hallowed turf, or for other diversions for the rest of the family such as sailing, fishing, climbing and trekking, leaving us to get on with the important thing — THE GAME.

And what a pleasurable way of learning something of Scottish history and of Scottish characteristics as Hamilton presents them. His explanations of golf courses or links in relation to the life of the people and their towns is a joy. For the golf analyst, his clear and precise observations of the design and objectives of the course architects are a constant stimulation — and a side of golf that is, unfortunately, rather neglected.

Introduction

Scotland has more golf courses for her population than any other country in the world. Moreover, most of these courses are open to visitors. Two of the five Open Championship courses in Scotland are municipal links—St Andrews and Carnoustie—and two others, Turnberry and Royal Troon, have few restrictions. But the visitor will also find that many small towns in Scotland also have first class courses of championship quality on their great, natural links, and there is a wealth of smaller, sporty courses where holiday golf is enjoyed at its best. No other golfing nation has so many golf courses where a three-ball, two-bag sixsome is not frowned upon, and where the young can learn the game in peace. Moreover municipal golf in the larger towns and cities can be good, and is certainly cheap.

To pick some of the 400 or so Scottish courses for this book involves problems of selection. Those golfers who can cope with the championship links at Turnberry or Carnoustie on a windy day may feel boxed in on Bonar Bridge's short but delightful 9-hole course: conversely those who enjoy family golf at Carradale, may find Dornoch's long and famous links rather an ordeal.

Nevertheless, some selection is necessary and I have chosen those courses on which good golf can be enjoyed. To meet other needs, I have also mentioned local courses of interest, particularly as these courses may be quieter, or cheaper, or more suitable for family golf.

Throughout this book I have the visitor or traveller in mind, and if the course is difficult to find, I have given directions. Visitors and golf writers are often confused by the different names for some Scottish clubs, many of which have a local name and a proper name e.g. Rosemount (Blairgowrie) and Arbroath (Elliot), and an index is provided to help with these ambiguities. I have also been bold enough to choose a best eighteen links and inland holes in Scotland, plus some memorable sporty holes and a selection of others with the best views.

Only a general indication of the services to be expected at these clubs is given since these services change rapidly and vary with the season. Similarly I have included only a general indication of the regulations for play by visitors, since these also vary. For the famous private clubs, careful planning ahead is necessary to arrange a visit, which should be done through the Secretary. Many equally well-known clubs, usually those well outside the cities, are welcoming to visitors except at week-ends and on competition days in summer. Lastly, there are a gratifyingly large number of clubs who have few if any restrictions on visitors. Further details of these costs and regulations can be obtained in the Scottish Tourist Board's excellent and detailed annual pamphlet, *Scotland, Home of Golf*, or by telephoning ahead to the club. The Automobile Association's *Touring Guide to Scotland* is invaluable in giving details of activities other than golf.

Throughout this book, I have the golfer of moderate skills in mind: there are so many of us. Scotland is where golf started. It is still a golfer's paradise, and I hope this book conveys some of the enduring spirit of golf as it is played in Scotland.

David Hamilton
Glasgow 1982

History of Scottish Golf

Historians continue to dispute whether or not the game of golf originated in Scotland. Though the inhabitants of Holland may have played the game earlier, it disappeared from that country in the 1600s, and golf became a national sport and obsession in Scotland alone. All the major improvements in the game up until the twentieth century appeared first in Scotland, and it was from Scotland that the rules, players and designers of the modern game spread throughout the rest of the world.

Golf was certainly popular in Scotland in 1457, since James II had to pass a law discouraging it, encouraging archery instead of golf among those who would form the army. Thus, golf was popular with the common soldiers. But it is the golf of the rich that we know most, since only records of their lives survive. In 1503 King James IV bought expensive clubs from a bow-maker in Perth and other records of his expenditure show the payment of debts as a result of lost golf matches. The King and his nobles played with specially-made brittle wooden clubs and used expensive leather-covered balls stuffed with feathers (the 'feathery'). But the mass of the people probably used simple wooden sticks and balls made of wood or cork pierced by nails. After the Reformation, Sunday golf was one of the casualties in Knox's new Commonwealth, and much legal energy was put into stopping golf on the Sabbath, a taboo which is still occasionally found in Scotland today.

At first the prohibitions on Sunday golf were against golf 'at the time of the sermons', but later they became a total ban on Sunday golf. From these prosecutions we get the picture of a game popular with the ordinary people, and one played on the links in or near the towns. Other local punishments could be harsh: in 1637 the records of Banff record that a boy was hanged for stealing, among other things, two golf balls. The ordinary people played with primitive clubs and balls—'common golf balls' as they were called, whereas the noblemen played the 'lang game' possible with their expensive sophisticated equipment.

11

One of the most interesting sixteenth-century golfers was Mary Queen of Scots who was noted to have played golf in East Lothian rather too quickly after the death of Darnley in 1567, and the most distinguished seventeenth-century golfer was the great Montrose, who played golf on the day before and the day after his wedding in 1628. Nor did he rest then, since nine days after the ceremony, he sent to St Andrews for more golf balls and six new clubs as replacements for old ones.

The well-to-do golfers met regularly on the links as informal golfing societies. For them it was a winter game, when the links were less busy and their agricultural interests were less pressing.

The Courses and Clubs

In the seventeenth century, the Scottish golf courses became recognisable as allowing the game as we now know it. In 1625 the 'first hole' at the Aberdeen links is mentioned confidently in the town's records. Golf at that time was played only on the common land belonging to coastal towns and the golfers had to share this ground with many others—footballers at play, fishermen drying their nets, women drying clothes and the army at their exercises. Only the links were suitable for golf, and the rich and poor golfers mingled there. This mixture of players on the links later had one useful effect since the aristocratic golfers were prepared to fight and pay for the necessary legal battles to preserve this land for everyone's use. In the eighteenth and nineteenth centuries, the towns started to grow and the links became encroached on by the new houses and bustle of the enlarging towns. The ancient common lands of central Glasgow and Edinburgh and the coastal links at Leith, Leven, Aberdeen and elsewhere swarmed with people, and golf became not only impossible but dangerous also. The rich golfers solved the problem by moving away, purchasing land outside the town where they laid out for themselves private golf courses and where they could continue their golf in peace. The poorer golfers in the larger towns often lost their golfing ground but, in the smaller Scottish towns which did not grow so rapidly, they were luckier and the ancient golfing habits of the town could still persist on the municipal links. To this day, St Andrews, Carnoustie, Monifieth and other towns still have their old golf links starting from the middle of the town, land which has been used by all for golf since medieval times. The English 'artisan golfer' is almost unknown in Scotland.

In the eighteenth century the rich golfers who had always gathered informally on the links, formed themselves into 'clubs'. The first golf club in the world was that of the Honourable Company of Edinburgh Golfers, now of Muirfield, and which started at Leith in 1744, though the Royal Burgess golfers have a claim for an even earlier existence. The Royal and Ancient Golf Club of St Andrews was second to appear announcing themselves as the 'Society of the St Andrews Golfers' in 1754 and gaining their present title in 1834.

In the nineteenth century, several other changes occurred which led to the rapid extension of the popularity of the game. The first was that a Scottish golf holiday became popular, and the second was that balls and clubs became much cheaper. This popularity reached a peak with the patronage of golf by men such as Asquith, Earl Haig and Arthur Balfour, who regularly took a Scottish golfing holiday at St Andrews or North Berwick 'the Biarritz of the North'. They were followed by numerous English imitators from the rapidly expanding middle class, who also hired rather bemused caddies to help them through a round. Also helping in this expansion of Scottish golf was the rapidly spreading network of new railways within Scotland. When a line reached a town which possessed a course, golf prospered: where no course existed, one was built, often with a new railway hotel also. Lastly, the growth of new golf courses at the end of the nineteenth century was helped by new technology. Golf had previously only been possible where the grass was naturally short: hence it had been a winter game, and later only played in summer on the hard trodden links of the holiday coastal towns. In 1901 the *Golfers Handbook* could report a novelty—the new

13

inland course at Aberfeldy was able to be used in the summer, since the grass was kept short by 'mowing it'. Thus with the new grass-cutting machines, golf could expand inland into the parkland areas and even cleared heathland. Golf could move away from the links.

With this rise of Scottish golf came also the rapid expansion of golf in the Empire and North America. There it was helped not only by the grass-cutting machines, but also by the use of watering devices which allowed grass to grow in places unsuited to natural coverage. To meet these needs of the game abroad, notably in North America, Scotland provided a flood of emigrant golf course designers, clubmakers and professionals.

The Equipment

The main developments in early golf equipment also occurred in Scotland. The early feathery golf ball was still popular until 1850 and prior to this the skilled craftsmen passed on their methods from father to son. The Gourlay family at Bruntsfield and later of Musselburgh were the favoured ball makers. There were also many skilled Scottish clubmakers, but the McEwan family (also of Musselburgh) where the suppliers whose products then fetched the highest prices, as they still do in today's antiquarian markets. Only the well-off could afford this equipment. The balls were the most expensive item, since their life was so short.

About 1848 a revolution occurred in golf ball and golf club manufacture. New cheap and strong club shafts could be made with hickory imported from America, and a revolutionary new, cheap ball appeared. There is dispute over who first introduced into Scotland the 'gutty' ball, a ball formed out of malleable gutta percha. But there is no doubt about the effects of its appearance. Previously only those golfers who could afford the brittle clubs and the expensive short-lived golf feathery balls could play the skilled game, but after the gutty ball appeared, serious golf was open to all. The new ball caused dismay among the golf ball makers, and initially they failed to understand that the increased popularity of the game would sustain and encourage their other role as clubmakers, and create new work for them as teachers and 'professional' golfers. Initially the ball makers tried to boycott the new cheap ball and at St Andrews they searched the whins for lost gutty balls and burned them. Then came the hickory and the iron headed, unbreakable club. These new clubs and balls meant an expanding popularity of the game.

Scotland's last gift to club-making is hardly known now. In 1894 a Baberton golfer and blacksmith, Thomas Horsburgh, patented a steel shaft. But these clubs were not accepted by the Royal and Ancient Golf Club and only thirty years later, under pressure from America, was the modern shaft introduced. By then a new, more reliable golf ball had been invented. The Haskell ball appeared first in Britain in 1901, and soon displaced the gutty ball in popularity, though the new ball was more expensive. These new shafts and balls marked the end of the Scottish domination of the game—the Haskell ball and the steel shafts had come from America.

The Game

The early Scottish game was singles match-play, and a primitive handicap system is hinted at even in the earliest records. There were inter-club competitions from 1830 onwards. The earliest professional competitions were great challenge matches amongst the well-known clubmakers and professionals. For this, money was put up by aristocratic backers to reward the winners, and heavy betting on the outcome occurred. The most famous match was the great three-round challenge match played over three different courses in 1849 between the St Andrews pair Allan Robertson and Tom Morris who eventually beat the Dunns of North Berwick to win the considerable stake of £400. It was a match of sustained drama, since in the last leg the North Berwick golfers were four up with eight to play on their own course, but still lost.

In 1857, the Prestwick Club organised an inter-club amateur tournament in which twelve clubs participated. But a second initiative of the Prestwick Club three years later was to be their most famous, namely the holding of an 'open tournament' for professionals, later to be known as 'The Open Championship'. The idea must have come from their pride in having attracted 'Old' Tom Morris from St Andrews to be their professional for a while, and the first of these tournaments at Prestwick in 1860 was of three rounds over 12 holes.

Old Tom and his son 'Young' Tom dominated the early years of this tournament, often recording astonishing scores over the rough courses and in spite of the use of the older equipment. From 1872 onwards, this tournament steadily grew in importance, and the Amateur and the Open for professionals were often played on the same course in the same week. Later the Open became sufficiently prestigious for amateurs to join in. The Open Championship left Scotland for the first time in 1894, thus recognising the rise of golf in England. Indeed the last win by a home-based Scot had been by Willy Auchterlonie in 1893, and the last win by a Scots-reared professional was in 1920, when George Duncan, born in Scotland and playing in England, won at Deal. Tommy Armour, who played little golf in Scotland, the land of his birth, returned from America to win at Carnoustie in 1931.

The Designers

As the game of golf spread first to England and then to America, the new players looked to Scotland for men to teach golf, make golf clubs and lay out their new courses. This task fell naturally to the Scottish professionals, but not always with successful results.

But 'Old' Tom Morris was popular and consistently successful and endeared himself to the owners of the land for a new course by remarking on his arrival that 'surely Providence had intended this for a golf links'. The professionals were successful in other directions. 'Young' Willie Park of Musselburgh was the first to exploit his potential in the way to be familiar later. After skilfully promoting himself as a golfer, using flamboyant dress and golfing challenges, he had a remarkably success-ful career as a businessman, club-maker and designer. At one point he had offices in Edinburgh, London and New York. His magic putter was skilfully advertised, but was difficult to use. Of the emigres, 'Young' Willie Dunn had early success in Europe. The Vanderbilts discovered him in Biarritz and took him to America, where he is still remembered for his design of the Shinnecock Hills course. Other Scots emigrants took their enthusiasm for golf with them. In 1902 a Mr John Duncan from North Berwick opened 'the largest golf store in the world' in New York. In 1901 a Scottish gold miner constructed a rough course at Cripple Creek, near Denver. The course was at 10,060 feet, and he wrote home claiming his links to be the highest in the world. No one disputed this.

At home, successful Scottish professionals could still make a good living from design of the courses for the many new clubs springing up throughout Britain. In Scotland the great golfer James Braid made his mark by laying out many of the new courses, and his total in Britain exceeded all others. Grateful committees often named one of the holes in their new course as 'Braid's Brawest' in his honour. In the north-east of Scotland Robert Simpson of Carnoustie and Archie Simpson of Balgownie had similar success and were in demand as designers.

A substantial reputation for course design was obtained by Donald Ross who left Scotland for America in 1898 and became well known as a designer there. While still in Scotland he had remodelled his home course at Dornoch and there he incorporated the features that were to set new standards. These ideas he used widely and they are much admired in his American work, notably in the lay-out of the Pinehurst No 2 course.

In 1890 there was a significant event. Some Scots golfers opened a club and course at the Hague. Golf had returned to Holland after centuries of disuse.

The Rules

The first rules of golf were, of course, devised in Scotland. The early game of golf was singles match-play, and in a match between gentlemen any disputes could doubtless be harmoniously resolved. However, the appearance of the Honourable Company of Edinburgh Golfers in 1744 meant also the organisation of a competition for their new silver trophy, and made necessary some form of adjudication of disputes.

Their first idea was to appoint one person for one year whose main function was to give judgement in disputes and he was called the 'Captain of the Golf'. But later the Honourable Company went further and drew up a set of rules for their competition. These rules were later copied by the Royal and Ancient Golf Club of St Andrews and from then on the R & A increasingly took over the initiative from the Edinburgh golfers, to the extent that they still, together with the United States Golfing Association, organise the rules of golf and give final judgements thereon.

In some ways Scotland lost the leadership of golf in the early twentieth century. Certainly Scottish golfers and golf courses no longer dominated the increasingly sophisticated game. But to regret this decline is to misunderstand the essential nature of Scottish golf. It started as the popular, economical sport of the people played on common land. This 'good golf' is its greatest tradition, and as I hope this book shows, it is a tradition which continues today.

Scotland and the language of Golf

Because golf evolved to its present form almost entirely in Scotland, many golfing terms have their origins in the Scottish language, as testified by the numerous words ending in –ie

Caddie: Though this word is probably French in origin (meaning the youngest sons of the nobility), it was soon changed to be applied to some disreputable porters who hung about the Edinburgh streets in the early eighteenth century. To them naturally fell the odd jobs and errands of the town and they also took on the work of carrying the golf clubs of the noble Edinburgh golfers—hence the modern usage of the word.

Bunker: The word was used by Sir Walter Scott to describe the shallow hollows used by sheep for shelter. Doubtless the word was also used for similar hollows on the golf links, which gathered in the running ball. The bunkers would tend to be deepened and lose their grass as a result of the repeated shots made from them, particularly when iron clubs became popular. These sandy hollows became the modern bunkers. They have been placed in all types of course.

Links: A term used mostly on the east coast of Scotland to describe the common land of the town used for recreation, military exercises and drying of clothes. The name may have come from the word 'lynch' — a ridge. The 'links' were not only found on the coast, since the term was used for the land at Bruntsfield in the centre of Edinburgh. The playing of golf on these links led to the term being applied to the golf course itself, but when golf expanded inland in Scotland, the name was restricted to mean a sea-side golf course.

19

Green: Originally the name was used in Scotland for the grassy area near a house. It may then have been applied to the flat area used for pall-mall or other stick and ball games, and then later to the entire playing area for golf. Later, as the quality of the golf courses improved, it was applied to the putting area only. The older, wider use of 'green' still survives in the phrases 'Green Committee' and the 'Rub of the green'.

Stymie: This old Scots word for a partially blind person was easily applied to the situation on the putting green when one golfer's ball lay between the other ball and the hole. This called for an ingenious shot in the days prior to the abolition of the stymie in 1949.

Dormie: A term used in match play when a player is leading an opponent by the same number of holes left to play.

Jigger: This narrow-bladed, short club was specially designed to play the traditional pitch and run shot of Scottish links golf. It was invented by Ben Sayers of North Berwick, and, though not favoured by professionals, it can still be lethal in the hands of a handicap player.

Mashie: An older term for an iron club, possibly about a No 5 in modern terms. Its pulping effect on the leather-covered feathery ball may have given it this name.

Niblick: An older name for a lofted, narrow-headed iron club designed originally to get out of ruts: about a No 8 in modern terms.

Feathery: The original golf ball made of expensive materials. It had only a short life before bursting and releasing the feathers. It was succeeded by the gutty ball in about 1848.

Gutty: This cheap successor to the feathery ball was made out of gutta percha. It immediately produced a revolution in the game of golf, since it allowed the game to be played by a much wider section of the community.

Brassie: In the mid-nineteenth century the tracks and paths beside and through the Scottish links became changed to hard, paved roads, notably at Musselburgh. To play from these unyielding surfaces the players had to strengthen and protect one of their soft-headed wooden clubs by adding a brass plate. This change proved to be useful also for ordinary shots and the plate was added to all woods thereafter. The name 'brassie' was kept for the equivalent of the No 2 or 3 wood.

Playing the Game

Beginners or visitors may run into difficulties with the unwritten rules and procedure of the game. Here are the main ones; most are international but some are Scottish.

The Honour: (i.e. the person playing first). In match play, the challenger plays first, i.e. the person named first in the draw: in medal (stroke) play the order is as on the written starting sheet. If in doubt, the lowest handicap player plays first, and a guest is invited to strike off first in a friendly match.

In a four-ball, one partner of the team of two has the honour for his team during the first nine, then their order of play is usually reversed. However, the winning team may often decide not to risk a change of honour at the 9th.

In a three-ball match the honour only changes after one player wins a hole outright: the displaced player then plays last of the three. There is no change after a halved hole, and, paradoxically the player who came third may still retain the honour.

Medal Play: Count the strokes played—this is the *Gross* Score: the *Net* Score results from subtracting the handicap from this Gross Score. Remember—the *Gross* Score is the *Greater* one.

Stableford Competition: The player plays against the par of each hole. For the round, the player receives ⅞ of his or her handicap, taking these strokes at the holes indicated on the card. Points are gained at each hole thus: *par* 2 points, *bogey* (one over par) 1 point, *birdie* (one under par) 3 points, etc. This replaced the older 'Bogey' competition in which simply the holes up or down relative to par were recorded, after allowing for handicap.

Singles Match Play: The weaker player is allowed ¾ of the difference in handicaps, and the strokes are given at the appropriate holes marked on the card.

Four-ball Match Play: The lowest handicap player receives no strokes. The three other players are each allowed ¾ of the difference between their handicap and that of the lowest handicap player. These players get their strokes at the appropriate hole.

Two-ball Foursomes: Often called 'Scotch' foursomes, the two members of the team play alternate shots with one ball as do their opponents. This method of play is fast and sociable. As golf has become slower, this two-ball game has had a modest revival, having always been popular in Scotland, notably with the Muirfield golfers.

In playing the game, the teams can be matched so that no strokes are given or taken. Otherwise the handicaps of each team of two are combined and ⅜ of the difference between these totals allowed as strokes at the appropriate holes. In a *greensome* match all four players drive, but only the best drives of each team are played.

Three-ball Matches: Strokes are allowed as in a four-ball. The winner of a hole scores 4 points, the runner-up scores 2. Thus six points are allocated per hole and in a two- or three-way tie, the tied players score 3 or 2 points respectively. For the honour in a three-ball match—see above.

Betting: Though betting is officially discouraged, most players enjoy a small stake on match play and most clubs add an optional sweepstake to their competitions. In foursomes or four-ball matches it is well to clarify the stakes in advance, since the phrase 'a ball a corner' may risk losing one or two balls according to local custom. A *Nassau* bet involves a stake on the match and a smaller stake on the result of each of the two nine holes: these bets serve to sustain the interest throughout the match. Similarly, a *press* may be agreed at the start, in which a player who is two holes down at any point may terminate the match, concede the bet, and a new match starts for double the stakes.

It is traditional to play the 'byes'—the holes remaining after a match is finished—for a smaller stake.

Lastly, interest may also be sustained throughout medal or match play by gaining small sums for golfing triumphs such as *Birdies* (one under par), *Oozles* (the person whose tee shot is nearest the hole at the short holes), *Ferrets* (holing out an approach shot from off the green) and *Golden Ferrets* (holing out from a bunker).

It is customary for the winner of the match to stand the first round of drinks at the 19th hole. A hole in one is generally thought to oblige the player to stand one drink to all golfers in the clubhouse on return to the clubhouse, but a bottle of whisky divided among the well-wishers may now suffice.

Dress and Play

The visitor to Scotland should be prepared at all times for *sun* or to meet *biting winds* and *rain*. But to be dressed for one usually ensures the other. The ancient Scottish golfing dress of heavy tweeds and plus-fours are out of fashion, but can be sensible on occasions. Play in Scotland can still be fast, and the visitor may find that a full set of clubs and a large bag may be a hindrance: a slim pencil bag, as used by many locals, may be more suitable.

North American visitors are often astonished and perplexed to realise that in many of the golf clubs a jacket and tie must be worn in the public rooms, notably the dining room and bar. Though the reasons for this rule are obscure it is nevertheless strictly enforced.

In Scotland, club *handicaps* are decided on the player's best rounds, played from the back tees on competition days. In other countries, all rounds may count and the average scores are used for the handicap. Scottish hosts should therefore not be contradicted when they say that a visitor's handicap is too high. Visitors will also understand why in Scotland a card is not usually marked by locals and match-play is preferred to stroke play in friendly games. Thus it is not customary to hole out when losing a hole badly. Visitors will note that this enables rounds of golf to be completed in under four hours.

Lastly, to protect the nation's health, *electric carts* are discouraged in Scotland: on producing a certificate of ill health or longevity, however, such a buggie may be produced.

The Scottish Weather

Many visitors are apprehensive about the weather in Scotland. While it is not true that the climate is continuously wild, wet and cold, it should be remembered that our temperate climate and adequate rainfall created the fine grass of the links which allowed invention of the original game of golf. Local weather reports are available on the telephone by dialling the appropriate number which can be found in any directory under Telephone Information Services. For those who wish exact figures on the Scottish weather the facts are given below: but on any particular day anything can happen.

'Lovely day,' said the nervous new American Consul-General to Scotland on his first visit to the links.

'Aye, but it's early yet,' said his host.

	Sunshine (hrs.)			Rainfall (ins.)		
	April	July	Oct	April	July	Oct
Turnberry	155	155	83	2.3	3.4	5.0
North Berwick	145	170	87	1.4	2.7	2.6
Carnoustie	140	154	104	1.8	3.2	3.3
Nairn	137	141	94	1.7	3.0	2.8

	Temperature (°F)			Annual Days of Snow
	April	July	Oct	
Turnberry	46.2	58.5	50.1	5.8
North Berwick	45.3	58.9	48.8	10.8
Carnoustie	44.8	59.0	47.9	9.3
Nairn	45.3	58.1	48.3	14.6

Source, *Atlas of Britain*, Clarendon Press, Oxford

These figures show that the west coast has warm sunny weather in the spring and that the east coast has fine golfing days well into the autumn. The figures also confirm that Nairn and the Moray Firth, though in the north, have a low rainfall. The warm

Gulf Stream means that the west coast is best suited to winter golf.

Buchan's Spells: Last to be considered are Buchan's cold and warm spells. Buchan was a late-19th century Scottish meteorologist whose collection of data allegedly suggested that regular spells of unseasonably good or bad weather occur throughout the year in Scotland. According to him the periods to choose, or avoid, for golf are:

Cold Spells: February 7–14, April 11–14, May 9–14 and November 6–13.

Warm Spells: June 29–July 4, August 6–11 and December 3–14.

Summer   Winter

THE COURSES

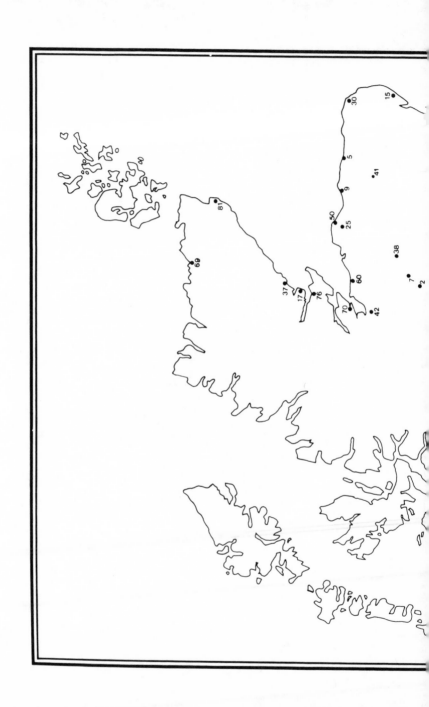

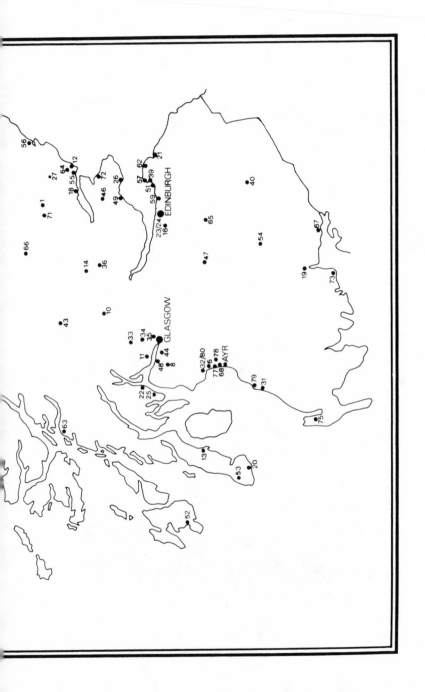

1. Alyth Pitcrocknie, Alyth, Perthshire
TEL: Alyth (082 83) 2268

Visitors: Visitors are generally welcome. Starting times can be booked ahead.

The Course: 6268 yds   SSS 70   Designed by James Braid, the course was opened in 1894. This is a well kept compact moorland course with a fine new clubhouse and good first hole. The drive at the second must be accurate, and the 4th and 5th have plateau greens. Perhaps the best hole is the long 11th (510 yds), sloping gently to the right throughout. The 18th green is large and joins the practice putting green. Fairways are flat, the rough is kindly and the greens now have a water supply. In former days, a branch railway line dropped members off at the first tee.

To get there: The course is well outside Alyth: take the B954 road eastwards from the town.

Neighbouring Courses: *Rosemount* (71), *Forfar* (27) and *Kirriemuir*—a course designed by Braid with its splendid short 17th hole.

2. Aviemore Dalfaber Village, Aviemore, Inverness-shire

Visitors: Restricted: co-owners of adjacent houses may have priority.

The Course: Aviemore, in its time as a sleepy holiday resort, had a 9-hole course which was sacrificed to build the commercial Aviemore Centre. This loss was regretted by all, but ambitious plans to build a championship course to add to the amenities of the development never came to pass. However, in 1982, a new start was made and the 9-hole Dalfaber Village course was opened north of Aviemore as part of Scotland's first planned housing and golf complex.

The course runs on moorland with birch trees lining each hole. Holiday chalets and homes are discreetly placed at the edge of the course. The fairways are narrow, and hence the course can be tight to play.

To get there: Signposted to the north of Aviemore.

Neighbouring Courses: To the south are *Kingussie* (45) and *Newtonmore* (61). To the north is the reviving course at *Carrbridge* and the established and delightful club at *Nethybridge*. The fine *Boat of Garten* (7) club is also near, as is the course at *Grantown-on-Spey* (38).

Other Activities: The area has major facilities for tourism and sport. River and loch fishing are excellent and there is climbing, walking and a gliding school. A swimming pool and ice rink are found at the Aviemore Centre.

3. Balgownie

(Royal Aberdeen Golf Club) Balgownie,
Bridge of Don, Aberdeen
TEL: Aberdeen (0224) 702571

Visitors: By arrangement with the Secretary or Professional.

History: The club was formally set up in 1780, but records of golf on the links in Aberdeen go back to 1589, and there are even hints of the game being played in 1565. This club is the sixth oldest in the world, and there are many historical golfing items preserved in the clubhouse. Before 1888, the club played on the links in Aberdeen, but after overcrowding became a problem, they moved to Balgownie. In a former day, a railway line conveyed members from Aberdeen to near the course. The club drew up a set of rules early in the history of the game and in 1783 they were first to introduce the 5-minute limit on searching for a ball.

Recently they have been firm in preserving the old ways, particularly of dress, and ladies were excluded from the clubhouse until 1970. The club published their bicentennial history in 1980, *200 Years of Golf 1780–1980* Aberdeen.

The Course: 6404 yds   SSS 71   A hidden chasm in front of the first green sets the mood of these stern long links. The ground is uneven but the landing areas for the drives are more level. After the 6th, the gorse closes in, compounding the golfing challenge. At the north end the course touches the Murcar links. It is usually more difficult to score on the second nine than the first. Little is seen of the sea, though it is close, as is the tradition on east coast links.

There is a relief (or 'ladies') course of 15 holes, and the Aberdeen Ladies clubhouse is nearby.

Best Hole: 9th — see 'Best Holes' p. 130.

To get there: On A92 north of Aberdeen, turn right down Links Road at Bridge of Don.

Neighbouring Courses: *Murcar* (58) is close by. The ancient municipal *King's Links* are to the south in Aberdeen, as are the popular municipal parkland courses at *Hazlehead*. The well-designed course of the *Deeside* club is to the west of the town,

Other Activities: Pony trekking, swimming and even skiing on an artificial slope are available around Aberdeen as is fine fishing, both at sea and in rivers and lochs.

4. Ballater
Ballater Golf Club,
Victoria Road, Ballater,
Aberdeenshire
TEL: Ballater (0338) 55658/55567

Visitors: Welcome: a starting sheet operates in summer. The Royal Deeside Golf Week is popular, and is held in the first week in May.

The Course: 6106 yds   SSS 69   The original 18-hole course was opened in 1906 with a great exhibition match between James Braid and Harry Vardon. The holes are laid out on the sandy land of the valley of the River Dee. The fine mountains which surround the town give an attractive setting to the course and there is a good clubhouse.

To get there: Easily found on the west of the town.

Neighbouring Courses: There are 18 fine and scenic holes at *Braemar*; the *Aboyne* course is set on a hillside and the attractive links at *Banchory* are laid out through pines beside the river. The Queen has an exclusive nine holes at *Balmoral*, and there is one of the most pleasant 9-hole courses in Scotland at *Tarland*, placed in stately surroundings.

Other Activities: The Dee valley offers good walking, climbing and salmon fishing. A famous Highland Games is held here in August. There is a gliding school at Dinnet.

5. Banff (Duff House Royal Golf Club)
Barnyards, Duff House, Banff, Banffshire
TEL: Banff (02612) 2062

Visitors: Welcome with some restrictions; there are many summer competitions.

History: Accounts of golf on the Moray Firth stretch back to earliest recorded times. A boy was convicted and hanged at Banff in 1637 for stealing golf balls, and in 1733 there is reference in the records of the Banff Magistrates Court to the 'first hole of the links'.

The early golf of this town was played on the seaside grass but as the town expanded and erosion and other sports threatened the links, the golfers withdrew to the parkland round the splendid, but empty, Duff House, gifted to the town in 1906. The course was subsequently redesigned by Dr. Alastair McKenzie.

The Course: 6161 yds   SSS 69   Though near the sea, the turf is of a parkland quality and the course heads inland beside the River Deveron. The fine trees of the estate are a feature.

To get there: The course is easily found on the east side of the town beside the main road. The name of the club is printed boldly on the roof of the clubhouse.

Neighbouring Courses: *Royal Tarlair* at Macduff has wonderful seascapes and *Cullen* has one of the sportiest courses in Scotland, finding its way up and down the cliffs of the rocky coast.

Other Activities: Salmon and trout can be fished for in the Deveron and there is safe bathing on the sandy beach.

6. Barassie (Kilmarnock Golf Club)
Hillhouse Road, Barassie,
Troon, Ayrshire
TEL: Troon (0292) 311077/313920

Visitors: Restricted: enquire ahead.

The Course: 6457 yds   SSS 71   The course was built as a coastal club for relaxation by the merchants of Kilmarnock in 1877. The links resemble those at Old Prestwick, not least for the marvellous compactness of the design, which still maintains each hole as an individual unit. The Gailes burn is a persistent hazard at five holes, and the 15th hole (220 yds) is highly regarded.
The club is used as a qualifying course when the Open Championship is in Ayrshire.

To get there: The turn-off to Barassie is well marked on the Irvine to Troon road (A78), and the club is beside the railway station.

Neighbouring Courses: The great links of Ayrshire are all handy— *Glasgow Gailes* (32), *Western Gailes* (80), the *Troon* courses (77, 78), and *Old Prestwick* (68).

7. Boat of Garten

Boat of Garten Golf and Tennis Club,
Boat of Garten, Inverness-shire
TEL: Boat of Garten (047983) 282

Visitors: Welcome. There are open competitions in the summer, including a popular 36-hole open event on the first Saturday in August.

History: The course was laid out by James Braid and it reflects his genius. The railway line formerly owned by British Rail is next to the first hole. It has now been restored by the enthusiasts of the Strathspey Railway, and trains link the village with the main line at Aviemore. There is now a large and hospitable modern clubhouse.

The Course: 5637 yds   SSS 68   Some consider this to be the most enjoyable inland course in Scotland and a supreme test of accurate golf. There is an individual setting for each of the holes which are often cut through birch wood or on moorland terrain. The first hole is short which sensibly helps to get play going. The 2nd hole is typical of this great course—slightly dog-legged, with a downhill drive but a second shot to be hit up to a tilted green framed by gorse. At the 5th the birches close in. The 380-yd 6th is possibly the most challenging hole in Scotland for the handicap golfer. It starts with a drive down from an elevated tee into an avenue through a birch wood. The drive must reach the turn of the dog-leg to get sight of the well protected plateau green to the right. Only two perfect shots can gain a par. The transverse fence has now gone from across the 10th fairway and most locals play short of the gully at the 15th rather than try to carry it. All that remains is to keep the ball in play off the eighteenth tee, no mean feat: even then the concentration cannot be relaxed, since the second shot to the eighteenth green is one of the most testing on the course.

To get there: Take the road through the village from the south and turn right at the former railway bridge.

Neighbouring Courses: There is an attractive course at *Grantown on-Spey* (38) and also the recently improved holiday course at *Carrbridge*. Nearby is the Abernethy club at *Nethybridge* with its famous 111 yd 2nd hole played over the road to Tomintoul. The old Aviemore and Kincraig courses no longer exist. The abandoned Rothiemurchus holes can still be found by enthusiasts near the road to the ski slopes, the former clubhouse being used as a centre for outdoor activities. The unmet demand for golf in this area is satisfied to some extent at Aviemore by the new nine-hole course at *Dalfaber Village* (2).

Other Activities: Two tennis courts are adjacent to the course, and there is a remarkable range of leisure facilities in the Spey valley.

8. Bridge of Weir

(Ranfurly Castle Golf Club)
Golf Road, Bridge of Weir, Renfrewshire
TEL: Bridge of Weir (0505) 612609

Visitors: Restricted: enquire ahead.

The Course: 6276 yds   SSS 70   The first hole leads from the clubhouse up to the fine turf of this moorland course which keeps in good condition throughout the year. The 170 yd 5th is a fine short hole set high above the Clyde. The broad green is not deep and when the pin position is moved further to the right it gives an increasingly difficult shot over treacherous country. At the 16th hole there is a fine panorama of the mountains to the north and west, and an indicator board naming the peaks is found beside the tee. The 18th is a splendid romp back downhill to the tall clubhouse.

To get there: Difficult to find, two-thirds of a mile up the hill of Prieston Road from the railway station.

Neighbouring Courses: *Old Ranfurly Golf Club* is 600 yards away and *Kilmacolm* (**44**) is in a neighbouring village.

9. Buckie (Strathlene Golf Club)
Portessie, Buckie, Banffshire
TEL: Buckie (0542) 31798

Visitors: Freely welcome. There are many open tournaments in the summer, including a four-day Open with scratch and handicap sections.

The Course: 5957 yds   SSS 69   Set to the east of the town, the course has a fine new clubhouse, and the exposed links have tough grass and peaty soil. Three of the holes converge on the hillock in the middle of the links. The last four holes, set in a narrow, inland part of the course make an exciting finish for stroke or match play, since they test accuracy rather than strength.

Best Hole: 17th — See 'Best Holes' p. 130.

To get there: Easily found beside the coast road to the east of the town.

Neighbouring Courses: Buckie's *Buckpool* course is close, at the west end of the town; the huge clubhouse includes some squash courts. *Cullen's* remarkable course, hanging on the cliffs, is further to the east on the Moray Firth.

Other Activities: There is a swimming pool in the town, and fine sea bathing.

10. Callander Callander Golf Club,
Callander, Perthshire
TEL: Callander (0877) 30090

Visitors: Welcome.

The Course: 5204 yds   SSS 66   Designed by Tom Morris in 1913, this course is sometimes compared to Gleneagles. It is laid out on moorland among fine pine trees and there are impressive views of Ben Ledi from some of the holes. The course returns to the clubhouse at one point. Scoring here can be difficult and straight tee shots are essential.

To get there: Signposted in the town.

Neighbouring Courses: To the south, the popular *Aberfoyle* course, now 18 holes in length, is found. Its original, charming, clubhouse has been preserved.

Other Activities: Fishing, sailing, trekking, canoeing, water-skiing and walking are well organised in this area.

11. Cardross
Cardross,
Dunbartonshire
TEL: Cardross (038984) 213

Visitors: Welcome on weekdays.

The Course: 6466 yds   SSS 71   The higher part of the course was extended into land bought from the adjacent monastery, but this area is under threat. The beautiful turf is of parkland type and the views from the top of the course are remarkable. The 340 yard first hole is a gracious start to the course. Beginning beside the Lower Clyde estuary it is sensibly arranged with bunkers to left and right and climbs gently uphill all the way. Underclubbing of the second shot is likely. The course also includes two famous downhill drives at the 7th and 18th holes. There is a large hospitable clubhouse, and the club is a great asset to the district.

To get there: Clubhouse is on the north of the main road in Cardross.

Neighbouring Courses: The *Helensburgh* course, which crosses back and forth on the moor above the town, is nearby. Also on a moor is the sporty *Vale of Leven* (Alexandria) 9-hole course with its dramatic surprise at the 1st hole. The flat municipal links at *Dumbarton* are popular locally.

12. Carnoustie
Carnoustie, Angus
TEL: Carnoustie (0241)53249 (Starter's Box)

Visitors: Welcome, since these are municipal links. There are numerous competitions organised here for visitors, including the Open Championship. There is a modern clubhouse close to the first tees, and numerous small private clubhouses, golf shops and hotels adjoin the famous links.

History: The first record of golf at Carnoustie dates from 1527 when Sir Robert Maule 'exersisit the gouf, quhan (when) the wadsie (wager) was for drink'. At the beginning of the 20th century the town of Carnoustie achieved another kind of fame, by sending out numerous local golfers as teachers and professionals to North America, the most notable being Stuart Maiden, the teacher of Bobby Jones. The Open Championships at Carnoustie have always given a special kind of excitement and when Henry Cotton won in 1937 with his famous round of 65, the new Dunlop ball was named after the astonishing score. Tommy Armour, a Scots emigrant from Edinburgh to U.S.A., came back in 1931 to win here from José Jurado who wrongly thought that a safe 5 at the last hole was all that was needed to win. Hogan, determined to win in 1953, arrived a week early to practise, and won the title. He was given a ticker tape welcome back to New York.

The Course: 6809 yds SSS 74 The championship links, the adjacent Burnside Course, and the new third course are owned by the town. There is still a special railway station which serves the links. The 1st hole has humps and hollows reminiscent of St Andrews or Old Troon, but bigger. Johnny Miller said it looked like the burial ground of 100 elephants, but the rest of the course is flatter. The 2nd hole has a famous and controversial 'penal' bunker—Braid's bunker—placed within driving range in the middle of the fairway. After Jack Nicklaus drove out of bounds at the 6th hole in the 1968 Open, he kicked his bag of clubs out of his caddie's hands but then started the charge that almost defeated Player. The 6th (570 yds) was the longest championship hole in Scotland. The 10th hole ('South America') commemorates the fate of a drunken would-be emigrant to that continent who collapsed there in a bunker after his farewell to the town: he changed his mind about leaving in the morning. The 14th has the famous 'Spectacles' bunker in a hillock at 400 yds from the tee. The terrors of the short 16th (235 yds in the 1975 Open) are dependent on the direction of the wind, and threaten a bogey for even the tournament leaders. The 17th is crossed twice by the Barry Burn, and forms a stern challenge at a crucial stage in any match.

Unlike other links the Carnoustie course changes direction frequently. For the 1975 Open it was extended to 7101 yds, though the 18th was shortened to a par 4 to increase the challenge and drama of the finish. In 1968, the course was at the longest ever for any Open Championship—7252 yds.

Best Hole: 17th — see 'Best Holes' p. 130.

To get there: Easily found: follow signposts in Carnoustie.

Neighbouring Courses: *Panmure* (64), and the *Monifieth* links (55) are near, as are the ancient windswept links at *Arbroath*.

Other Activities: Sea angling and bathing are good here and near Arbroath are cliffs and caves of interest. There is a gliding centre at Condor.

13. Carradale Carradale, Argyll
TEL : Carradale (05833)624
(Secretary)

Visitors: Welcome; there are summer competitions.

The Course: 3240 yds   SSS 63   This is one of Scotland's best
known sporty 9-hole courses and countless children first learnt
their golf on holiday here. The short links are laid out on
moorland shared by sheep and other grazing stock. The design
here breaks normal rules of golf course construction, but this
only adds to the enjoyment. There are some very fine holes, with
splendid views of Arran. If an approach shot hits a sheep fence
round a green, the shot may be taken again. The club does not
own the land on which the course runs, and there have been
recurring crises recently over the playing rights here.

To get there: Easily found behind the hotel.

Neighbouring Courses: *Dunaverty* (20) and the championship
links at *Machrihanish* (53) are to the south. *Tarbert* and
Lochgilphead are to the north.

Other Activities: The harbour encourages sailing, and there are
fine forest walks. Sea and loch fishing are popular.

14. Crieff Crieff Golf Club, Ferntower, Perthshire
TEL: Crieff (0764) 2397/2909

Visitors: Welcome.

The Course: 6362 yds   SSS 70   Situated in the popular resort area of Crieff near the famous Gleneagles courses, is the new Ferntower Course. It first opened for play in August 1980 and extends below a southern facing slope called the 'Knock', a familiar local landmark. This new course comprises 11 completely new holes and some from the original 18-hole course, nine of which now make up the shorter but nevertheless delightful Dornock Course. In addition to its beautiful turf and its invigorating highland air, Crieff offers magnificent views over the Strathearn valley. Bounded by the A85 Perth Road, both courses run in an east–west direction. The long par 4 seventh and twelfth holes can be particularly challenging. The modern rotund style professional shop at the first tee is the object of admiration by its many visitors.

To get there: Easily found on the A85 north of the town.

Neighbouring Courses: At *Comrie* there are nine holes laid out on lush parkland, and their clubhouse has some interesting golfing relics. *Gleneagles* (36) with its four golf courses is nearby.

Other Activities: There is a sailing school at Loch Earn. Fishing is available on the River Earn and the Loch. Crieff Hydro has many leisure facilities including a swimming pool, squash and riding stables.

15. Cruden Bay

Cruden Bay Golf and Country Club,
Cruden Bay, Aberdeenshire
TEL: Cruden Bay (077981) 2285

Visitors: Admitted freely: some weekend restrictions.

History: The course was designed by Tom Simpson and was built for the holiday visitors brought by the new railway which reached here at the turn of the century. This line is now closed and the hotels are quieter, but the rise of caravan holidays and the oil boom have prevented any decline in popularity of the course.

A country club has been added which provides overnight accommodation. Eric Brown, Scotland's best known professional in recent years, was attached to this club at one time.

The Course: 6401 yds   SSS 70   The drive from the 1st must be held to the left against the slope to the right. The 2nd green is easily held if the perils of the mischievous fairway are avoided. The beautiful short 4th hole is near the old fishing village of Port Erroll and the 6th green is surrounded by numerous difficulties of various kinds. The famous 8th is reminiscent of the design at Dornoch's 2nd hole, since a ridge running to the green diverts the ball left or right into bunkerless valleys. The course climbs up on to the cliffs at the 9th and descends back again at the 10th, but only at the narrow 14th is the fine beach seen at last. The 17th has a raised green, again reminiscent of Dornoch. A relief 18-hole course (*St Olav*) is placed inside the original course. Tom Simpson said that the 1st, 8th and 18th at Cruden Bay are in his best 18 holes in Britain.

Best Hole: 8th — see 'Best Holes' p. 130.

To get there: The club is easily found in the village.

Neighbouring Courses: *Peterhead* has 18 holes: there are sporty 9 holes at *Ellon* and a fine natural links at *Newburgh* beside the famous salmon fishing estuary: the *Aberdeen* courses are 20 miles to the south. At *Inverallochy* medal play can start at either end of these ancient links, and those beginning at the south end of the links send their cards back by car to the north end. The famous fishermen golfers of Inverallochy were the last players in the world to give up the gutty ball.

Other Activities: There are fine beaches and good river and loch fishing.

16. Dalmahoy Kirknewton,
Midlothian
TEL: 031-333 1845

Visitors: Admitted freely.

History: The course was designed by James Braid and the clubhouse was a country house designed by Adam and owned by the Earl of Morton. The original private golf club was taken over for redevelopment as a country club in 1978 and now provides a variety of sports facilities over a 1000-acre estate. Many of the original members rejoined the club after the changes.

The Course: *East Course* 6645 yds SSS 72; *West Course* 5212 yds SSS 66 The layout of the courses is unchanged from the original design. The East Course which is now regularly used for championships makes good use of the varied countryside and the fine woodland. The 430 yard 7th hole, backed by the Adam clubhouse is the most spectacular and best hole on the course. There is a hidden surprise of a broad chasm over which the second shot has to be flighted to the green. In tournaments this hole is played as the 16th as the front and back nine are reversed in order to allow a tougher finish and also to improve television coverage. There is an ample practice area and putting green.

To get there: On the A71, 7 miles west of Edinburgh.

Neighbouring Courses: *Ratho Park's* course is also constructed on an old estate, and the *Baberton* and *Torphin Hill* courses are to the east.

17. Dornoch (Royal Dornoch)
Dornoch, Sutherland
TEL: Dornoch (086281) 219

Visitors: Few restrictions: bookings can be made. There are many open tournaments for visitors in summer including a popular Golf Week. The modernised clubhouse is large and comfortable: a number of hotels are beside the first two holes.

History: Records have been found which suggest that golf was played here in 1616. The modern era began in 1886 with a new lay-out designed by Tom Morris on these natural and spacious links. Improvements were made later by Donald Ross, a native of Dornoch who lengthened the course to suit the Haskell ball. Ross some years later left for America and there designed almost 300 golf courses, including the famous Pinehurst links. His brother Alex won the U.S. Open. Dornoch's 15th hole was copied by Ross for the Columbus Ohio Golf Course, and many other American courses show features of his style. Herbert Warren Wind puts Dornoch in his top six courses of the world and its situation in the north-east ensures that it is not over-played by admiring golfers. The course is also favoured by fine dry weather in summer, and the quiet town is very hospitable.

John Sutherland was the famous secretary here for fifty-three years from 1883, and used the increasingly challenging course to revive the fortunes of the town. He also raised many generations of fine amateur golfers and the Wethereds learned golf here during their Dornoch holidays.

There is a short history of the club—Donald Grant *Personal Memories of Royal Dornoch Golf Club 1900–1925.*

The Course: 6533 yds SSS 72 Donald Ross's design is seen in every hole and particularly round the greens. His hallmarks are huge greens and a series of devices—bunkers, ridges, hollows and plateaus—to prevent a loosely hit ball from running on to the green.

The straightforward 1st hole introduces the golfer to the superb greens, and a Donald Ross ridge short of the 2nd green often prevents a par and shows what is to come. The 3rd and 4th have hump-back or sloping fairways which have to be reached diagonally from tees placed above on the raised beach. The course turns for home at the 9th and the 12th (500 yds— 'Sutherland') named after their famous secretary, still gives the player nightmares long after it is played. Sloping left to right and turning left uphill, it is only reached after a series of brave shots against the natural slopes and into the prevailing wind. The 14th has been widely praised, but it is only of delight to those who take a medium iron to play the second shot to a 459 yard par 4. The course then proceeds on to the top of the raised beach at the 16th and at the 17th tee the player has an odd choice between a long drive into a valley and hence losing sight of the green, or playing short. The 18th green, like many others, is guarded by a ditch which looks natural enough, but was probably dug by Ross himself. The rough is not fierce, nor does it need to be.

There is a relief 9-hole course (the **Struie**), which was part of the main course before it was reorganised.

Best Hole: 4th — see 'Best Holes' p. 130.

To get there: Easily found from the east side of the square.

Neighbouring Courses: *Brora* to the north has a natural links with broad sand bunkers and erosions, and *Tain* (76) and *Golspie* (37) are within reach. *Bonar Bridge* has an attractive and quiet moorland 9 holes above the town.

Other Activities: There is a famous beach, trout fishing at Buidhe Loch, and hill walking.

18. Downfield
Turnberry Avenue
Dundee
TEL:
Dundee (0382) 825595

Visitors: Restricted and confined to weekdays: phone ahead.

The Course: 6872 yds   SSS 73   This championship course was constructed for the people of Dundee in 1964, and has fine parkland turf cut through mature woodlands. For major tournaments the order of the holes are changed and the 9th becomes the 18th. The wide generous fairways of the first nine are followed by shorter and tighter holes towards the finish. The best hole on the course is the 485 yard 11th. It has a small green guarded by water and many bunkers.

To get there: Not easily found. Take the ring road to the north of Dundee, turn north at the Timex building up Staffa Road, then left into Harrison Road.

Neighbouring Courses: There are fine municipal courses at *Caird Park* and *Camperdown Park*. *Monifieth* (55), *Panmure* (64) and *Carnoustie* (12) are on the coast to the east. *Scotscraig* and *St Andrews* (72) are easily reached over the Tay Bridge.

19. Dumfries

1. Dumfries and Galloway Golf Club
TEL : Dumfries (0387) 3582

2. Dumfries and County Golf Club
TEL : Dumfries (0387) 3585

Visitors: Some restrictions: enquire ahead.

The Clubs: Two clubs are found in this prosperous town. Both have rather similar lay-outs on rolling parkland, and both have elegant clubhouses with small car parks. The **Dumfries and Galloway Golf Club** is of 5782 yds (SSS 68) and the **Dumfries and County** is of 5909 yds (SSS 68). The D and G is more open to visitors than the D and C.

To get there: Watch for sign posts. The D and C is just to the south of the town centre, and the D and G is a mile or so to the north-east on the A701.

Neighbouring Courses: The south-east of Scotland has numerous sporty courses and the championship links at Southerness (73) are close. Visitors are also welcome to the well-kept 18 holes belonging to Chrichton Royal psychiatric hospital in Dumfries.

Other Activities: There is pony trekking, river, loch and sea fishing. A gliding school operates at Kirkgunzeon. There are a number of nature reserves.

20. Dunaverty (Southend)
Southend, Argyll
TEL: Southend (0586)
3937 (Secretary)

Visitors: Welcome without restriction.

History: This remarkable links course was extended to 18 holes some years ago, and a new clubhouse built in 1976. Golf connoisseurs are delighted to find that there are still electrified fences round the greens to keep off the sheep, but regular golfers here do not notice. Should the fence be hit by the ball, the shot may be played again. Golf at Dunaverty has been affectionately described in the books of Angus MacVicar who lives within an iron shot (or two) of the course. The club's most famous golfer is Belle Robertson, the Curtis Cup player and winner of many national tournaments.

The Course: 4597 yds SSS 63 The turf is similar to the neighbouring course at Machrihanish, but some say that the views from Dunaverty are better. The visitor has to master shots to the small lush square greens. Much of the course is compactly placed in traditional links land, and the many changes in direction of the course please purists in matters of golf design. The downhill shot at the 11th must be one of the most thrilling drives in all Scottish golf.

To get there: Signposted from the main road in Southend.

Neighbouring Courses: *Machrihanish* (53) is to the west. The sporty 9-holes at *Carradale* (13) to the north break all rules of design but generations of young West of Scotland golfers were taught the game here without harassment.

Other Attractions: There is a splendid beach, and fine fishing locally, plus many hill walks. There is also an indoor swimming pool in Campbeltown.

55

21. Dunbar Dunbar East Links Golf
Club, East Links, Dunbar
TEL: Dunbar (0368) 62317

Visitors: Welcome.

History: This area is one of the ancient sites of Scottish golf history. In 1616 two men of the neighbouring parish of Tyninghame were censured for playing 'at ye nyneholis' on Sundays and in 1640 a local parish minister was censured for similarly playing at 'gouf'. In 1794 a group of gentlemen in Dunbar, with strong masonic ties, formed a club which played at Westbarns, to the west of the town, but this foundered some years later. In 1856 the present club was formed and started play at the present course. In 1890 the Honourable Company of Edinburgh Golfers decided to leave Leith and considered a site near Dunbar, but chose Muirfield instead later.

For a thoughtful history of golf at Dunbar, see R. C. Brownlee *Dunbar Golf Club: a Short History* Dunbar 1980.

The Course: 6441 yds   SSS 71   Three holes are played on the south of the beach wall and then the course continues back over the wall on the narrow links beside the sea and rocky beach. At the 9th hole, Barns Ness lighthouse is a feature, and at the 14th green is seen The Vaults, a listed building which is preserved from removal or improvement.

To get there: Easily found to the east of the town.

Neighbouring Courses: To the north is *North Berwick* (62) and the great courses beside *Gullane* (39). Until 1939 there was golf at the ancient site of Westbarns to the north-west of Dunbar.

Other Activities: There is a fine beach and good sea fishing. There is also a local nature trail and a nature reserve.

22. Dunoon (The Cowal Golf Club)
Ardenslate Road, Kirn,
Dunoon, Argyll
TEL: Dunoon (0369) 2216

Visitors: Welcome with a few reservations. Open tournaments are held in the summer.

The Course: 6251 yds   SSS 70   Rising high above the Clyde, this course gives fine views of the estuary and of the shipping movements there. The first few holes climb uphill and call for testing shots to the square hidden greens. The turf can be heavy even at the highest point of the course, and there is a splendid downhill drive at the 12th.

To get there: Turn west in middle of town. There is a ferry service to Dunoon from Gourock, and golf parties travelling to the Cowal Golf Club can obtain reduced fares.

Neighbouring Courses: *Innellan* to the south has a sporty 9 holes and shares, with *Blairmore and Strone* to the north, a claim to the best views in Scottish golf. Neither course is recommended for those with cardiac conditions, but otherwise golf here may be therapeutic.

Other Activities: There is sea fishing and boating, plus loch fishing at Loch Eck. The Forestry Commission has an Arboretum at Kilmun.

23. Edinburgh – Barnton

(Royal Burgess Golfing Society)
Whitehouse Road, Edinburgh
TEL: Edinburgh (031) 339 2075 (Secretary)
339 2012 (Clubhouse)

Visitors: Restricted: enquire ahead.

History: Here plays a club which is one of the oldest in the world, and some have claimed it to be the first golf club ever. The original members played at Bruntsfield Links and eventually settled at this beautiful parkland area on the edge of Edinburgh. In a formar day a railway adjacent to the course transported the members to and from Edinburgh, and a bell was rung in the clubhouse bar to warn members of the train's departure.

The Course: 6604 yds   SSS 72   The quality of the turf and greens and their upkeep are of the finest. This, plus the length of the course, has made it a frequent venue for tournaments. The 4th hole is considered to be the best here, since at 464 yds and with a narrow entrance to the raised green, a par is not easily obtained.

To get there: Take A90 to the Barnton roundabout on the west edge of Edinburgh.

Neighbouring Courses: The equally famous *Bruntsfield Links Golfing Society*, at Davidsons Mains, is adjacent. Many other Edinburgh and Lothian clubs are also nearby.

24. Edinburgh – Braids

Braid Hills Approach, Morningside
Edinburgh 10
TEL: Edinburgh (031) 447 6666

Visitors: Admitted freely: Saturday play can be booked ahead on Fridays in summer, but there is no Sunday play. Some private clubs play over the courses.

History: Public golf in Edinburgh was formerly on the Bruntsfield Links nearer the centre of Edinburgh. The golfers of Edinburgh relinquished their legal right to play on the overcrowded links when the Edinburgh Corporation in 1911 agreed to build these courses on the Braid Hills instead. Though James Braid was a member here, the courses are not named after him.

The Courses: Braids No. 1: 5731 yds   SSS 68; Braids No. 2: 4832 yds   SSS 65   Though these rugged hills are an unlikely looking area for golf, the holes are beautifully laid out along the natural lines of the land. The different lengths of the two courses allow a choice of golf for all and from the top of the hills there are magnificent views of Edinburgh, the Lothians, Fife and the Firth of Forth. In winter a composite course is constructed from the two courses.

The **Edinburgh Dispatch** tournament has been played here for many years and the courses are beautifully maintained.

To get there: Take the A702 out of Edinburgh, turning left into Braid Hills Road when the hills are reached.

Neighbouring Courses: The parkland *Mortonhall* course is close, as is *Craigmillar Park*. Many other Edinburgh and Lothians clubs are also nearby.

25. Elgin (Hardhillock Golf Club)
Hardhillock, Elgin
TEL: Elgin (0343) 2338

Visitors: Welcome. There are many open tournaments in the summer.

The Course: 6421 yds   SSS 71   This moorland course has a tricky start beside the road to Grantown, and the length of the 1st hole, the small green at the second and the trees at the 3rd all add to the difficulties. After a hope of a 3 at the short 4th, there is the splendid long and difficult 485 yard par 5 5th. This hole has a dramatic drive out into space, where the ball hangs long enough for the prevailing wind to carry the shot towards the rough and bunkers on the right. The second shot has also to be long to set up the delicate chip to the small high green—a vital shot which is often left short.

The course is well laid out and maintenance is excellent. The clubhouse is commodious and meets the needs of the many visitors.

To get there: Easily found beside the A941 south of Elgin.

Neighbouring Courses: *Lossiemouth* (50) is close, as are all the fine links of the Moray Firth.

26. Elie (The Golf House Club)
Elie, Fife
TEL: Elie (033) 330301

Visitors: Welcome with some restrictions.

History: Records of golf on these links date from 1589, but the game may have been played here even earlier. In a famous lawsuit in 1812, the golfers' right to play on the links was upheld against the wishes of the landowner. In 1884, one of the first ladies golf clubs in Scotland was formed here, and there has always been a second club—the Earlsferry Thistle—which had an artisans' membership. James Braid was born here but walked to Leven to play his early golf, though later he joined the Thistle club. The course has been used for the World Seniors Tournament.

There is a delightful history of the club—Alasdair M. Drysdale *The Golf House Club, Elie* Elie 1975.

The Course: 6253 yds SSS 70 Many consider this to be the most enjoyable of the Scottish links courses. It has remarkably lush turf and the beautiful bunkers, with their deeply coloured sand are set well down into the fairways. In good weather, Edinburgh and the North Berwick coast can be seen from the course. The links suffered, like many others, in the droughts of the 1970s, but the club successfully employed a St Andrews water diviner to find a new supply of water for the course. The water found is more palatable than the town supply and local golfers fill their flasks from a tap at the 6th to add to their whisky.

The opening drive is blind and a periscope, saved from the submarine 'Excalibur', allows the starter to check on progress over the hill. The course finds its way behind the town out to Chapel Ness, then round the bay towards MacDuff's Cave and back to the town, with the golfing challenge increasing after the turn.

To get there: Follow signposts in main street.

Neighbouring Courses: *Lundin Links* and *Leven* (49) are to the south. The famous *Crail Club* at Balcomie has retained an older style of layout, and it was here that internal supporting iron rings for the holes were first introduced. A celebrated lawsuit by the Crail golfers in the last century also confirmed their right to play on the common land at Balcomie. These events are described in James G. Dow's book *The Crail Golfing Society 1786–1936* Edinburgh 1936.

Other Activities: This area has a full range of enjoyable sports—pony trekking, fishing and sailing.

27. Forfar Cunninghill, Forfar
TEL: Forfar (0307) 65683

Visitors: Welcome.

The Course: 6055 yds SSS 69 This fine moorland course has views over to the Braes of Angus. It is rapidly changing in character, since the pines planted in 1947 are converting each hole into a separate unit. There are frequent changes in direction and the tees and greens are beautifully constructed. The course, designed by James Braid, contains one of the many 'Braid's Brawest' holes in Scotland. This is the 375 yard 15th, where there is a choice of lines from the tee, the left being the safest, and the right the shorter. Sandy Saddler, the former Walker Cup captain has made the name of this, his home club, well known.

To get there: Take the A932 east out of Forfar and turn right on to the A958. The club is two miles outside the town.

Neighbouring Courses: The *Brechin* course to the north is constructed on flat land outside the town and the course has now been divided by the new by-pass. *Carnoustie* (12), *Panmure* (64), *Monifieth* (55), *Kirriemuir* and the Dundee courses are all within reach.

Other Activities: There is hill walking and fresh water fishing is particularly good in this area.

28. Fort Augustus

Fort Augustus, Inverness-shire.
TEL: Fort Augustus (0320) 6333 (Secretary)

Visitors: Welcome.

The Course: 5154 yds   SSS 66   The 9-hole course laid out by James Braid is kept in immaculate order, and must be one of the neatest 9-hole courses in Scotland. There is an ancient wooden clubhouse and an honesty box. This highland village boasts a central cricket pitch, a Benedictine monastery and a Catholic boys' school: otherwise it is a typical Scottish community.

To get there: Easily found on south of the village.

Neighbouring Courses: Like other parts of the west coast, there is a lack of golf in this area. *Fort William* (29), *Oban* (63) to the south, and *Inverness* (42) to the north are the nearest clubs.

Other Activities: The area is rich in all water sports—fishing, sailing and canoeing. There are many fine walks and climbs plus two nature trails.

29. Fort William

Torlundy, Fort William, Inverness-shire.

TEL: Fort William (0397) 4464

Visitors: Welcome.

The Course: 6218 yds   SSS 71   Opened for play in 1976, the moorland turf of this course has taken time to settle. It is beautifully designed, and provides a serious test of golf in an area which previously had no course within reach. The first half of the course is long, with two holes over 500 yards, but with two holes under 100 yards the overall yardage is kept low. One of the best holes on the course is the 287 yard 1st. This short par 4 requires a drive over a valley, leaving a tricky approach to a tiny green. There is a fine new clubhouse, and the whole course is overlooked by Ben Nevis. The mountain path to the North Face starts here.

To get there: On the main road to the north of the town.

Neighbouring Courses: Other than *Spean Bridge's* 9-holes there are none within easy reach, but *Fort Augustus* (28) is to the north, and the remarkable hills and valleys of the *Oban* course (63) are to the south.

Other Activities: Ben Nevis (4406 ft) is Britain's highest mountain and has both easy and difficult ways to the summit. Sea fishing is popular here and loch fishing is also available.

30. Fraserburgh

Fraserburgh, Aberdeenshire.
TEL: Fraserburgh (03462) 2287

Visitors: Welcome.

The Course: 6216 yds SSS 70   This town's coastal links were surely designed for a golf course. The entire course now lies between the coast road to Peterhead and Fraserburgh Bay, with high sand dunes at the edge of the links. The four fine holes to the south of the road, which were formerly part of the links, can now be used for a brief few holes or a warm up for the game. The first two holes mount to a vantage point which gives a splendid view of the fine finish to the course and the dunes, bay and fishing town beyond. A good score has to be made early: the finish is tough.

To get there: Easily found beside the B9033 to Peterhead.

Neighbouring Courses: *Peterhead* is to the south and east, and the historic links at *Inverallochy* are close by.

Other Activities: The beach and bay are popular for swimming and sailing. There is a choice of loch fishing and splendid sea fishing from the pier.

31. Girvan Girvan, Ayrshire

TEL: Girvan (0465) 4272

Visitors: Welcome.

The Course: 5078 yds   SSS 65   The first eight holes begin from a starters box placed on the ancient links and make their way along a windy tight coastal strip. Fine views of the volcanic plug of Ailsa Craig are obtained, and out to sea the diving gannets and coastal shipping are a feature.

At the 9th hole the course turns inland on to lush parkland beside the Water of Girvan. The course finishes beside the clubhouse which is set back a little from the first tee. At the 15th hole a long drive is required to carry the River Girvan.

To get there: Signposted in the centre of town.

Neighbouring Courses: *Turnberry* (79) is nearest to the north, and the Ayrshire courses are all reachable. *Stranraer* (75) to the south is also close.

Other Activities: Sea fishing from the pier is popular and there are boats for hire and sea trips available. In the town there is an indoor pool, tennis and bowls.

32. Glasgow Gailes

Gailes, by Irvine, Ayrshire
TEL: Irvine (0294) 311347

Visitors: Restricted: enquire ahead.

The Course: 6432 yds   SSS 71   The Glasgow Club is unique in owning two courses, one at Killermont in Glasgow and this one at Gailes on the coast. Players on the waiting list for membership of the Glasgow course can play at Gailes, and there is also now a small local membership. The course is used for the qualifying rounds of the Open when held at Royal Troon or Turnberry. The 2nd hole (340 yds) is perhaps the best challenge to golfing skill as the drive must be placed accurately on to a fairway which narrows and is uneven. The second shot tends not to run on to the sloping green which is surrounded by hollows and rough.

The mild coastal winter weather ensures that the course is rarely closed, and the Glasgow golfers continue their play here all year round. The course is a typical links and the heather lining most holes is a persistent hazard. Conifer plantations are maturing and add to the attractive lay-out.

To get there: On the A78 main coastal road south of Irvine, take the Gailes turn-off.

Neighbouring Courses: *Western Gailes* (80) is over the railway line, *Irvine Bogside, Royal (Old) Troon* (77) and *Barassie* (6) are close by.

33. Glasgow – Buchanan Castle

Drymen, Glasgow. TEL:Drymen (0360) 60307

Visitors: Restricted: enquire ahead.

History: The fertile land round the Endrick Water used for this golf club was formerly a private race course, as the fence to the right of the 1st hole testifies. There is a prominent abandoned Castle whose roof was removed to avoid penal taxes. Eric Brown, Scotland's most celebrated professional golfer of modern times, was professional here for a time. The course was laid out by James Braid and was opened in 1936. There is a gracious and hospitable clubhouse.

The Course: 6032 yds   SSS 69   Though on flat land, the holes are of great variety with lush turf and the Endrick Water present throughout. There are fine views of Ben Lomond to the west and the Campsie Hills to the east.

To get there: Turn left off the Glasgow road just short of Drymen.

Neighbouring Courses: There is an attractive 9-hole course at *Strathendrick*, and the *Aberfoyle* course to the north has been improved and extended to 18 holes. Further north is *Callander's* (10) popular moorland course with its fine clubhouse and views of Ben Ledi.

34. Glasgow – Dougalston

Dougalston Golf Course, Strathblane Road,
Milngavie, Dunbartonshire
TEL: Glasgow (041) 956 5750

Visitors: Welcome. This is one of the few courses near Glasgow which is not a private club: hence visitors are encouraged.

The Course: 6694 yds   SSS 72   This beautiful, long and testing course was recently constructed and cut through mature birch and pine woods. This has meant that each hole is individual and very attractive. The 2nd (360 yds) is perhaps the best looking hole in Scotland, particularly in May when the rhododendrons are in flower. There is an added hazard at this hole as a fine pine tree stands in the middle of the fairway. The fairways narrow at the point to which the drive reaches and the water hazards also can create problems.

To get there: Signposted on the Milngavie-Strathblane road.

Neighbouring Courses: All the Glasgow clubs are to the south and the fine course at *Buchanan Castle* (33) is to the north.

Other Activities: Hill walking in the Campsies and there is fishing nearby. Glasgow has a full range of other attractions for visitors.

35. The Glasgow Golf
Club Killermont, Bearsden, Glasgow
TEL: Glasgow (041) 942 2011

Visitors: Restricted: enquire ahead.

History: The club was formed in 1787, but the forebears of the original members played golf on Glasgow Green for centuries previously. The records show that the magistrates allowed golf on the Green in 1624 and even the earlier the Kirk Session had prohibited golf in Blackfriars Yard in 1589. The club had varying fortunes, and frequently moved as a result of the town's growth; finally they purchased their present home at the gracious estate of Killermont. The club is unique in also owning another course at *Gailes* (31) on the Firth of Clyde, which offers splendid links golf even in winter. The Glasgow Club's Tennant Cup is the oldest open amateur tournament in the world.

The Course: 5970 yds   SSS 69   The ancient trees between the fairways on this beautiful parkland course are a feature as are the fine greens. The course, laid out by Tom Morris, changes direction repeatedly, returning to the stately clubhouse at a number of points. The members do not allow the rough to grow to a penal length. The best hole on the course is the 530 yard par 5 5th. This is a deceptively difficult par 5 which changes direction twice. Old and new trees are also hazards and the safe line is first to the right then to the left, which lengthens an already long hole. Many members have to be content to score a six here.

To get there: Hidden to the north of Maryhill Road where this road crosses the Kelvin river at Garscube estate.

Neighbouring Courses: All courses in Glasgow are handy, notably *Buchanan Castle* (33), *Bearsden, Dougalston* (34), *Milngavie* and the two courses at *Hilton Park*.

36. Gleneagles

Auchterarder, Perthshire
TEL: Auchterarder (07646) 3543

Visitors: Welcome in general, but hotel guests may have precedence and 4-ball starting times are limited. Booking ahead is possible and sensible.

History: The two championship courses were laid out by James Braid and the Prince's course was extended to 18 holes in 1974. A fourth course (the Glendevon) has recently been added in this, one of Scotland's most beautiful golfing areas. Though not used often for major tournaments now, the courses are popular for televised matches, and the immaculate green-keeping and superb condition of the fairways are widely admired. There is a local golf club with a small membership who have some privileges on the courses. There are many expensive time-sharing and other types of holiday homes nearby attracted in by the golf.

1. King's Course: 6504 yds   SSS 71   The grand and noble scale of the hills, fairways, bunkers and greens of this course makes the judgement of length and height difficult, particularly at the 1st. The holes are well separated from each other and the splendid views, isolation and wildlife give the course a unique atmosphere. The 390 yard 17th is a great tactical hole which is only conquered with caution, as television matches from this beautiful course have shown. Though not long, the hole is surprisingly difficult, and if the drive overshoots the point of the dog-leg to the left, the ball ends up down a steep bank and the score mounts. The 18th affords magnificent views over the valley to the Ochil Hills with the stately Gleneagles Hotel in the foreground.

2. Queen's Course: 6278 yds   SSS 70   This course is shorter but of the same quality as the King's. Dog-leg holes are a feature and the 13th and 14th holes are much photographed.

The two courses make a good pair for a day's visit and further variety can be obtained by playing on the shorter **Prince's Course** (4678 yds). The new **Glendevon Course** is longer (5762 yds) and has more hazards, notably at the 120 yard 1st hole played over the Laich Loch.

Clubhouse: Changing facilities are available, and there is a bar and restaurant. A few overnight rooms are available in the Dormie House. The Hotel offers lavish accommodation and food at appropriate prices, and has many leisure facilities. It is now open all year round.

To get there: Follow directions along the A823 off the main A9 Stirling to Perth road.

Neighbouring Courses: The local *Auchterarder* course is handy. The Perth courses are close and a good 18 holes are found at *Crieff* (14). The ancient golfing area at *Stirling* is to the south, with a full 18 holes on high parkland near the castle, and 9 new holes near Stirling University.

37. Golspie Ferry Road, Golspie, Sutherland.
TEL: Golspie (04083) 266

Visitors: Unrestricted.

The Course: 5852 yds   SSS 68   Golf here dates from 1889, and the present lay-out from 1905 and 1967. The 1st hole (formerly the 18th) sets the pattern for these pleasing links. The course proceeds along the sandy coast, then moves abruptly inland at the 7th hole. Six holes on moorland turf follow, and there is a final return to the pleasant links land, though the former Duke of Sutherland's eccentric statue on Ben Bhraggie catches the eye. The 9th (Paradise) is much admired by golfers in the North.

To get there: Turn off at the southern end of the main street in Golspie.

Neighbouring Courses: *Dornoch* (17) and the links at *Brora*.

Other Activities: The town is close to the sea and the mountains and there is an indoor swimming pool at the school.

38. Grantown-on-Spey

Grantown-on-Spey, Moray
TEL: Grantown-on-Spey (0479) 2079

Visitors; Admitted freely: there are Open tournaments in the summer, including a popular four day Open in August.

History: Robert Cruickshank, repeatedly runner-up to Bobby Jones in American golf between the wars came from Grantown. The course was designed by James Braid.

The Course: 5683 yds SSS 67 The first few holes make economical use of a flat triangle of land, but on crossing the road and moving east the course has six inspired holes reminiscent of Gleneagles. Of these the 410 yard 12th is the most notable. This is a noble hole cut through ancient Speyside pine woods and flanked by heather; the fairway narrows all the way to a small green. There is a testing and interesting finish near the clubhouse.

To get there: Turn east at the north end of the main street.

Neighbouring Courses: Quiet 9-hole courses are found at *Nethybridge* and *Carrbridge*, and there is the incomparable 18 holes at *Boat of Garten* (7). The fine links courses of the Moray Firth are not far away to the north.

Other Activities: The Spey river offers fine fishing and canoeing, and loch fishing is available in the area. Pony trekking is also popular.

39. Gullane Gullane, East Lothian

TEL: Gullane (0620) 842255
(Starter)

Visitors: Freely admitted, including Sunday golf: access to the clubhouse is restricted to those playing on No. 1 course. Play on the short course for children is free.

The Course: No. 1 (Championship) 6446 yds SSS 71; No. 2 6090 yds   SSS 69; No. 3 5004 yds   SSS 64   These three courses offer a graded test of golf, and attract many visitors. All three courses fan out from a roadside start in this attractive village. The holes are laid out on the same links and hill as the neighbouring Luffness and Muirfield courses. No. 1 course starts gently up Gullane Hill with an ingathering green at the 2nd hole: Lord Elgin suggested, and paid for, the filling in of this valley. The course then toughens, as does the wind, in the otherwise peaceful golfing paradise over the hill, with its fine views of the Firth of Forth, Fife, the Lothians and Edinburgh.

The No. 1, like the others, is beautifully maintained, and is used as a qualifying course in the Muirfield Open Championships. The British Women's Championship has been played here.

Recently, a Museum of Golf has been opened by Archie Baird, the well-known local golfer and collector. It is found beside the professional's shop.

To get there: Easily found in Gullane.

Neighbouring Courses: *Muirfield* (57), *Luffness* (51), *Longniddry* and the delightful hidden *Kilspindie* course, with its interesting clubhouse, goes down to the sea.

40. Hawick (Vertish Hill)

Vertish Hill, Hawick.
TEL: Hawick (0450) 2293/3238

Visitors: Welcome. Like many Border clubs, open tournaments are held here in summer.

The Course: 5929 yds   SSS 69   The course starts beside the ancient site used for the annual Vertish Hill sports. The first three holes climb slowly up a lush valley with the Nipknowes road to the right as a constant hazard. The course soon reaches the top of the Hill and from there remarkable panoramic views are obtained of the Borders' hills and towns. The fairways are broad and new pine trees have added to the attractiveness of the course. The last hole is a par 3 with a huge drop from the tee to the small double green shared with the first hole.

To get there: Take the Newcastleton road in the town.

Neighbouring Courses: The views from *Selkirk's* moorland course may be even better than from Hawick, and there is good golf at *Minto and Jedburgh* (9 holes). The new course at *Newcastleton* is to the south.

41. Huntly Huntly, Aberdeenshire
TEL: Huntly (0466) 2643

Visitors: Welcome: there are summer competitions.

The Course: 5393 yds   SSS 66   This beautiful parkland course beside the Deveron has prospered as a result of careful attention and improvement. Set in a park belonging to the Gordons, the course was ploughed up during World War II. It was restored to 18 holes, and the new clubhouse and new trees are steadily improving the attractions of the course. The rough is kindly, but the broad ditch at the 1st hole and later may cause difficulties.

To get there: Find Cooper Park near the town's centre.

Neighbouring Courses: The *Turriff* course also runs on lush Buchan turf, and new trees have been added. The view from the *Old Meldrum* nine holes is so panoramic that a trig point has been constructed beside one of the tees. *Inverurie's* club prospers, as a result of a new clubhouse and its wide fairways. *Kintore's* moorland course also gives fine views to the east.

Other Activities: Fishing locally is of high quality, and there are many fine walks and local antiquities to visit. A bowling green is nearby.

42. Inverness

Culcabock, Inverness
TEL: Inverness (0463) 33422

Visitors: Welcome: there are many summer competitions.

The Course: 6226 yds   SSS 70   The course is set out on parkland high above the town. The club has prospered and the course and its upkeep are of high quality. Intelligent tree planting is now beginning to make each hole look more individual. The first ten holes are on parkland and the 10th hole follows the burn to the old mill. Then there are five holes across the road laid out on top of and below a raised beach, and ending with the fine difficult short 15th hole. The course then returns to the main area and ends with a long 18th hole.

To get there: Easily found on the Kingsmills road off the A9.

Neighbouring Courses: There is a remarkable choice of good golf to the north of Inverness. *Tain* (76) and *Dornoch* (17) are notable and to the east are the Moray Firth clubs, *Nairn* (60), *Lossiemouth* and many others. In the town are the *Torvean* municipal links and some therapeutic holes at *Craig Duncan Hospital*.

Other Activities: Loch and sea fishing are splendid in this area and there are forest walks.

43. **Killin** Killin, Perthshire
TEL: Killin (05672) 312

Visitors: Freely admitted.

The Course: 9 holes   2508 yds   SSS 65   In 1897 an employee of the Bank of Scotland in Killin described golf here on Finlaraig meadows. The club was founded formally in 1913 and may be one of Scotland's most picturesque golf courses. The first tee is in a splendid situation, particularly when the River Lochay is in spate. The 4th hole can claim two blind shots to the green. The 5th (519 yds) is downhill all the way back to the river, and is one of the most enjoyable holes in Scotland.

To get there: Easily found to the north of the village, on the A87 Aberfeldy road.

Neighbouring Courses: *Strathtay* and *Aberfeldy* are the nearest courses, and are of 9 holes each, as is the course at *St Fillans*. The gracious 18 holes at *Taymouth Castle* (Kenmore) are also worth a visit.

Other Activities: This is a fine area for walking and climbing and there is excellent fishing in the Lochay and sailing or canoeing on the Tay. There are some nature trails starting in Aberfeldy, and also one on Ben Lawers.

44. **Kilmacolm**
Kilmacolm, Renfrewshire
TEL: Kilmacolm (050587) 2139

Visitors: Welcome except at the weekends.

The Course: 5890 yds SSS 68 This village is proud of its moorland course with its fine views and memorable individual holes. The heathland rough can give difficulty and tee shots may have to carry over trouble. The 360 yard 3rd hole epitomises the spirit of this course which is one of Scotland's most enjoyable moorland courses. There is a fine downhill drive, from an unusually shaped tee, which must be followed by a bold shot to hold on the large undulating green. Skill rather than force is required to score well here as the course is not long.

To get there: Turn east off the main A761 road just south of the town centre.

Neighbouring Courses: *Bridge of Weir* (10), *Gleddoch House* (48), and the *Greenock Club* with its fine views of the Lower Clyde.

45. Kingussie

Kingussie, Inverness-shire
TEL: Kingussie (05402) 374

Visitors: Freely welcome, and the course is seldom crowded. Open tournaments are held in the summer.

The Course: 5468 yds   SSS 66   Even in this holiday valley, this well-kept course is not often busy although it offers much rewarding golf. Set on the hills above the Spey, there are fine views of Speyside and the Cairngorms. Many holes are on the lush parkland turf beside the Alt Mhor Burn, which is often a hazard. The rest of the course is on heathery moorland.

To get there: Signposted on the main A9 on entering the town from the south.

Neighbouring Courses: *Newtonmore* (61), *Boat of Garten* (7), *Aviemore* (2) and *Grantown-on-Spey* (38). For the history of golf in the Aviemore area, see the entry for *Boat of Garten* (7).

Other Activities: Pony trekking is organised locally and there is a wild-life park nearby. Loch Insh has small boat sailing and canoeing facilities.

46. Ladybank

Annsmuir, Ladybank, Fife.
TEL: Ladybank (03373) 0814

Visitors: Freely welcome.

The Course: 6617 yds   SSS 72   This fine, long, almost inland course, is laid out on flat terrain used in olden times as a military camp. Like the course at Rosemount, pines and birch line each hole, thus enclosing and separating them from each other. Heather forms the semi-rough. The great coastal golf courses of Fife are near and this course gives a contrasting golfing challenge. There is a new clubhouse, and the course is used for the qualifying rounds of the Open Championships when at St Andrews.

To get there: The club is signposted from a car park near the railway station.

Neighbouring Courses: *Leven* (49), *Lundin Links, Elie* (26), *Scotscraig* and the *St Andrews* (72) courses can be easily reached.

Other Activities: (see St Andrews)

47. Lanark

The Moor, Lanark, Lanarkshire
TEL: Lanark (0555) 3219

Visitors: Restricted to weekdays before 5 p.m.

History: The Club is one of the oldest in Scotland, and the course was laid out in 1851 by Old Tom Morris on an ancient golfing area also used for military camps. At one time a great railway hotel was planned here but Gleneagles was chosen instead. The Scottish qualifying rounds for the Open Championship have been held here in recent years.

The Course: 6415 yds   SSS 71   This is a moorland course with heathery rough, and is laid out on uneven terrain. Kept in championship condition it attracts many visitors. The 368 yard 1st is a fine hole, and a difficult one. To the right of the tee is rough ground and a cart track which has a seemingly magnetic attraction for the drive. The second shot has to be accurate and strong to gain the elevated green. The 12th (362 yds) is an attractive hole having a deep dip protecting the green. The course is one of the few in Scotland which finishes with a short hole, and the shots to the green can be viewed from the huge windows of the 19th hole.

To get there: The course is 1½ miles from the centre of the town. The road leads from the bus station at one end of the main street.

Neighbouring Courses: *Carluke* and *Carnwath* are closest. Some distance to the south is Britain's highest golf course at *Leadhills*.

Other Activities: There is a boating loch close to the course and a swimming pool in the town.

48. Langbank

(Gleddoch House Golf and Country Club)
Langbank, Renfrewshire.
TEL : Langbank (047554) 304

Visitors: Freely welcome.

History: This country club and golf course were built on Sir William Lithgow's estate and opened for play in 1974.

The Course: 6236 yds   SSS 71   The course rises high above the Clyde, and a feature is the narrow guarded entrances to the greens many of which are on two or three levels. The best hole on the course is the 181 yard 2nd. This downhill short hole has a fine view. A bunker guards the medal pin position and forces the safe shot wide, leaving a long putt to the hole. Each hole is different and at the controversial 11th and 13th the drive and second shots must land in islands of fairway between rough. The 17th and 18th run downhill from almost the highest point of the course, and they command superb views of the Vale of Leven and Ben Lomond.

The Clubhouse: A day ticket entitles visitors to use the numerous club facilities, which include two squash courts and a small swimming pool.

To get there: Take the Langbank exit from the M8 motorway along the Clyde.

Neighbouring Courses: *Gourock, Erskine* and *Kilmacolm* (44) are close.

49. Leven Links Road, Leven, Fife
TEL: Leven (0333) 23509

Visitors: Welcome.

History: These old links are the successors of even older golf links which existed nearer the centre of Leven at Dubbieside. The rapid expansion of shipbuilding there and other heavy industry plus the new railway, pushed the golfers westwards from Leven to their present home. Play in a former day was allowed to start simultaneously from the Leven and Lundin ends of the links, but it now starts only at the west end. The Leven Open Amateur Tournament might be the first open tournament in the world, a claim also made by the Glasgow Club for their Tennant Trophy. It is said that the introduction of boxes on the tees holding sand was first made at Leven and the modern hole-cutter was devised by their Captain in 1877. The course has been used for qualifying rounds when the Open Championship is at St Andrews, and the relief **Scoonie** course is nearby. A number of private clubs play over these public links. Some famous clubmakers were, and are, based in Leven, notably Nicoll and earlier the Patrick family.

The Course: 6426 yds   SSS 71   The course closely resembles St Andrews, since it runs over uneven links terrain. The 1st and 18th share a common fairway and an abandoned railway line runs through the middle of the course. The 18th green, with a burn running in front makes a fine finish. The tradition of the public links persists here, since a bowling green is also found beside the first fairway. Like the Old Course at St Andrews, the links at Leven can be played in reverse in winter, playing first to the 17th hole and so on.

To get there: Easily found on the shore road in Leven.

Neighbouring Courses: The well-known course at *Lundin Links* is to be found just across a drystone dyke to the west and the relief *Scoonie* course is nearby. There are good courses at *Kirkcaldy* and at *Dunfermline*. The *Alloa* course, with its fine views, has survived threats of purchase for redevelopment as housing. *Tulliallan* at Kincardine-on-Forth is a pleasant parkland course.

Other Activities: The area has numerous other attractions—a beach, sailing and fishing.

50. Lossiemouth
(Moray Golf Club)
Lossiemouth, Moray.
TEL: Lossiemouth (034381) 2018

Visitors: Welcome: there are many open competitions in Summer.

History: Lossiemouth is a friendly club and course for the people of the town. It was laid out in 1889 by Tom Morris and new holes were added by Henry Cotton in 1970. The modern tee box, with elevated legs, is thought to have been introduced first at Lossiemouth. The relief 9-hole course has now been extended to 18 holes and is called New Moray. It is partly enclosed by the original Old Moray. The old clubhouse has been modernised, and contains some fine old golfing pictures. There is also a 6-hole 'Baby Course'.

The Courses: Old Moray 6643 yds   SSS 72; New Moray 6258 yds   SSS 71   Both courses are laid out on natural links land which delighted Tom Morris when he first saw it. There is a fine beach and the courses nestle behind the dunes. The Old Course changes direction frequently and the greens are flat and fair. The start and finish of the Old Course must have the best setting of any in Scotland. The 17th green is the site of a famous incident since Asquith was attacked here, while on holiday, by militant suffragettes.

Best Hole: 18th — see 'Best Holes' p. 130.

To get there: Easily found in centre of town, and signposted from further away.

Neighbouring Courses: *Elgin* (25) has a parkland 18 holes of high quality, *Nairn* (60) and the *Forres* hilly parkland course are nearby. There is a sporty links at *Hopeman* close to Lossiemouth, with a fine sea view, but their famous railway carriage clubhouse has been replaced.

51. Luffness (Luffness New)
Gullane, East Lothian.
TEL: Gullane (0620) 843114

Visitors: Enquire ahead. The course is used for qualifying rounds of the Open Championships at Muirfield, and is a favourite with Edinburgh golfers.

History: The club was formerly known as Luffness Old. It played on land nearer the beach to the west, where the clubhouse was camouflaged by turf to avoid the ire of the irritable landowner Lord Hope. The club then split in two—one half going to Luffness New, the other to Kilspindie. The early history of golf in this area is recorded by the Rev. John Kerr: *The Golf Book of East Lothian* (1895), and this rare book fetches high prices in the antiquarian book world.

The Course: 6087 yds   SSS 69   After a few holes on the flat sandy land, the course climbs round Gullane Hill beside the Gullane links, and wide panoramic views of the Firth of Forth are found. There is a gracious clubhouse.

To get there: Found beside the A198, on the Edinburgh side of Gullane.

Neighbouring Courses: *Muirfield* (57), the *Gullane* courses (39 and *Kilspindie*.

52. Machrie (Islay Golf Club)
Port Ellen, Islay
TEL: Port Ellen (0496) 2310
(Machrie Hotel)

Visitors: Unrestricted. The modernised hotel serves as the clubhouse, and, out of season, green fees are placed in an honesty box in the adjacent farm courtyard.

The Course: 5964 yds   SSS 69   In a former day, the Machrie annual professional tournament attracted Taylor, Vardon and Braid to compete for the £100 prize, which was then the highest stake in the world of golf. There is still a very competitive summer amateur handicap tournament for the large, solid silver, Kildalton Cross trophy. A Golf Week with competitions and instruction is held in the spring, based at the adjacent hotel. The fine springy turf is reminiscent of Machrihanish, and both courses may owe something to the centuries of sheep grazing on the links. The course is laid out on uneven land, and traditionalists enjoy the blind shots to the greens, though the reorganisation of the course in 1978 removed many of these ancient features.

To get there: You can fly to Islay or take the car ferry from West Loch Tarbert. Once on the island, a lift to the course is often offered to those carrying golf clubs, or the Post Office van service can be used.

Neighbouring Courses: None. The nearest are on the island of *Tiree* and on the mainland at *Machrihanish* (53).

Other Activities: There are fine beaches, good fishing and many local antiquities to visit.

53. Machrihanish
by Campbeltown, Argyll
TEL: Machrihanish (058681) 213

Visitors: Welcome. There are many Open Tournaments in summer.

History: Tom Morris laid out the course in 1876 and on seeing the links round Machrihanish Bay, he said that 'providence had surely intended them as a paradise for the game'. Originally this was a club for the merchants of Campbeltown, who travelled across the peninsula by using the small railway. The railway has gone, the merchants are fewer, and the club is now entirely open. The design and upkeep of the course are of championship standard, and the club and clubhouse are notably hospitable to visitors.

A short history of the club is available—D. J. McDiarmid *1876–1976: 100 Years of Golf at Machrihanish* 1976.

The Course: 6228 yds   SSS 70   The unique quality of the turf—sandy, yet rich and springy—has been much admired.

The greens are large and sculptured and each hole is unique enough to be retained in the memory long after a visit. None is more remarkable than the famous first hole where the drive is played across the beach to reach the fairway. Wind, weather and ability have all to be computed before deciding how much of the angle can be cut off. The 2nd and 12th greens are very convoluted and the view of Jura while going up the 3rd is splendid—on a good day.

The 5th, 10th and 12th are full of golfing challenges. The controversial green at the 13th slopes steeply away from the player and the 14th and 18th have Dornoch-like dips in front of the greens. Like many Scottish links courses, the sea is near and can be heard but is seldom seen after the first hole.

The adjacent air base and weapon store touches the course at the 11th hole.

Best Hole: 1st — see 'Best Holes' p. 130.

To get there: The first tee is beside the main road (B843). There are daily flights from Glasgow to the air base.

Neighbouring Courses: The fine 18 holes of *Dunaverty* (20) at Southend are near: the sporty nine holes at *Carradale* (13) are ideal for family golf, and *Tarbert* to the north also has nine good holes.

Other Activities: There are forest trails nearby and pony trekking at Carradale. There is an indoor swimming pool at Campbeltown and sea bathing, fishing and skin diving.

54. Moffat Coateshill, Moffat
TEL: Moffat (0683) 20020

Visitors: Welcome with some restrictions. There is a popular Golf Week in the spring with tuition and competitions.

The Course: 5218 yds SSS 66   This moorland course high above the town is in a noble setting. There are panoramic views over the gracious town of Upper Annandale and to the mountains beyond. There is a distant sight of the lower Annan valley and the Solway coast. The 9th hole is placed above a sheer rock face. The course record is a score of 60.

The course here was laid out by Ben Sayers and opened in 1904.

To get there: Found to the west of the town.

Neighbouring Courses: *Dumfries* (19) is nearest, but is 20 miles away.

Other Activities: Moffat is a major holiday area, dating from its former fame as a spa town. There is fine walking, and fishing in the Annan is popular.

55. Monifieth
Princes Street, Monifieth, Angus
TEL: Monifieth (0382) 532767 (Starter's Box)

Visitors: Welcome but play at week-ends is restricted: a number of private clubs play on these municipal links.

History: In the 1890s, the ancient golf links of this east coast town were threatened by speculative building, and a grand Bazaar was organised, after which the ground was bought for the community for £4,000. Five clubs then played over the links, but the Panmure club departed for Barry in 1899, leaving the rest here.

The Course: 6657 yds   SSS 72   This is a championship course of championship length, kept in fine condition: when the Open Championship is at Carnoustie qualifying rounds are held here. The rather bleak east coast landscape has been softened by the addition of numerous intelligently placed pine plantations. The course starts and finishes in a narrow neck of land between the railway and the town. The 6th and 7th holes flirt with the railway and the burn. The 10th hole was damaged badly in the dry summers of the '70s and the fairway has been relaid. The Ashludie relief course (SSS 66) is tight, short, and beautifully laid out: in spite of recent changes, it still claims to be the most compact in Scotland.

To get there: Easily found on the railway side of the main street (A92).

Neighbouring Courses: *Panmure* (64) touches this course at the east end, and the *Carnoustie* links (12) are near.

Other Activities: There are beaches and fishing available locally.

56. Montrose Montrose, Angus

TEL: Montrose (0674) 2634

Visitors: Admitted freely: a booking sheet is available on the previous day at busy periods. The numerous private clubhouses close to the course are friendly to visitors.

History: There are records of golf played at Montrose as early as 1567, and at nearby Brechin in 1508 a golf club was recorded as used as a murder instrument.

This is a public golf links with attached private clubs, the oldest being the Royal Albert, founded in 1817. The course has been used for most of the major Scottish domestic championships.

The Course: Medal course 6451 yds   SSS 71   Like many other Scottish seaside links, the holes are set low between the town and the dunes, but a new tee has been built at the 6th hole which gives a fine view of the beach. The course changes direction frequently, a feature which pleases purists in matters of golf course design. There is an enjoyable relief course beside the main links, and an ample practice area.

Best Hole: 3rd — see 'Best Holes' p. 130.

To get there: From the centre of Montrose take the road to the beach.

Neighbouring Courses: *Edzell* and *Brechin* have 18 parkland holes, and there are the windy links at *Arbroath* (the Elliot Golf Club).

Other Activities: The fine beach, bay and Basin offer swimming, fishing, sailing and bird-watching. There is a nature reserve at St Cyrus.

57. Muirfield
(Hon. Company of Edinburgh Golfers)
Gullane, East Lothian TEL: Gullane (0620) 842123

Visitors: Only a handful of visitors with introductions are allowed per day and these slots are booked well in advance. Visitors are advised to have a caddie to help with local protocol on the course, particularly as local members playing two-ball foursomes can advance at remarkable speed. Four-ball matches are banned at busy periods and week-ends.

History: Muirfield is the home of the oldest golf club in the world. Founded in 1744, the Honourable Company of Edinburgh Golfers also drew up the first set of golf rules. They played first at Leith to begin with until they moved to Musselburgh and then in 1891 to Muirfield. The layout has been modified frequently and the quality of the course and its upkeep are internationally admired. The active membership comes mainly from professional and business circles in Edinburgh, and they do not encourage medal play, 4-ball matches, or women in the clubhouse. There have been many famous incidents in major tournaments on and off this course. Walter Hagen who was to win the Open here in 1929, put his second shot close to the wall at the 9th, and pulled out a left-handed club to deal with it. Cotton won the Open here in 1948 and Nicklaus triumphed in 1966. Trevino chipped into the 17th hole in the final round to beat an astonished Jacklin in 1972. Tom Watson won in style here in 1980. The course is highly regarded in the golf world: James Braid gave one of his sons the middle name of Muirfield, and Jack Nicklaus took the name for his new American club.

The club's history is given by a former member George Pottinger in *Muirfield and the Honourable Company* Edinburgh 1972. The clubhouse had an extension in 1981.

The Course: 6601 yds SSS 73 The course is lengthened for championships.

Muirfield is of a classic links type, though hints of a parkland character are detectable. It changes direction continually and can play long on a windy day. There is always an intelligent line from the tee: the greens are hard and fast. Clusters of fairway bunkers faced with turf are a feature, and the only way out may be backwards. The first nine holes enclose the second nine and the 10th tee is at the clubhouse.

The rough can be fierce, and a loose drive at the 10th ruined Palmer's bid for the Open in 1966. The championship tees can be seen behind the medal tees, and during the Open Championships here, the tented village is to the right of the first hole.

Best Hole: 9th — see 'Best Holes' p. 130.

To get there: At the southern end of Gullane village an inconspicuous road, signposted to Grey Walls Hotel, leads to the club.

Neighbouring Courses: *North Berwick* (62), *Gullane* (39) and *Luffness* (51). There was formerly a private 9-hole club on the east side of Muirfield (Archerfield) and the wood there was used in Robert Louis Stevenson's *The Pavilion on the Links*.

58. Murcar Bridge of Don, Aberdeen
TEL: Aberdeen (0224) 704345

Visitors: Welcome, but some restrictions.

History: The course was laid out by Archie Simpson of Balgownie with modifications later by James Braid. The club was the first in the north-east to allow Sunday golf, but only after a stormy debate and public controversy in 1910. As at other Aberdeenshire clubs, the seascape has been changed by the activities associated with North Sea Oil exploration. In a former day, a railway line and its 'Murcar Buggy' ran to the course from Bridge of Don to transport members from Aberdeen. During World War I the club disbanded, the course was used for agriculture and the clubhouse became a wireless station.

The Course: 6226 yds   SSS 70   The course is laid out on land adjacent to the Balgownie links, although there is more variety of terrain here and many views out to sea. The first four holes touch Balgownie and the 5th (162 yds) is a short hole over a canyon or two. The 6th and superb 7th lead to the turn. The 10th heads up on to higher ground. The drive at the 14th tends to go out of bounds and the 16th is a treacherous short hole.

Best Hole: 7th — see 'Best Holes' p. 130. Simpson, the golf architect, considered this as one of his finest holes.

To get there: Signposted on the coast side of the A92 north of Aberdeen.

Neighbouring Courses: To the south are *Balgownie* (3), the Aberdeen courses, and the peaceful 9 holes at *Newburgh* beside the beautiful Ythan estuary. To the north is *Cruden Bay* (15).

Other Activities: See *Balgownie*.

59. Musselburgh (Old Links)

Musselburgh, Midlothian.
No telephone.

Visitors: Freely admitted. A small green fee is sometimes collected if a local council official attends. There is no clubhouse, and the starting point is difficult to find.

History: These inconspicuous nine holes remain as a testimony to what was the centre of Scottish golf during its greatest era. Here played, in the mid 1800s, the Honourable Company of Edinburgh Golfers, the Royal Musselburgh Golf Club, the Royal Burgess Golfers and the Bruntsfield Golfing Society—some of the best known Scottish clubs, plus a large number of smaller societies. Not only that, but Musselburgh produced champion professionals like the Parks, Ferguson, Brown and the Dunns. The town was the centre of the golf ball and clubmaking industry for many years. Gourlay was the ball maker whose products were most sought after, and McEwan's clubs were supreme (and still fetch the highest prices in sales today). And it was the Musselburgh men that led the early spread of the game abroad, going out as professionals, golf course designers and club and ball manufacturers to reach all parts of the world. Musselburgh was the pace setter in innovation, including the introduction of the device to cut a standard 4¼ inch hole in the putting green (1829) and the invention of the metal plate on the 'brassie' wooden club (1885) to deal with shots from the new hard paved roads to the right of the first few holes. It was here that many of the great professional challenge matches took place, as did many Open Championships. But in the nineteenth century the success of the town and its golf meant overcrowding and overplaying of the links. The Edinburgh clubs decided to move once more to new private courses reached by rail: even the Open moved with the Honourable Company to Muirfield. The Musselburgh links deteriorated in the absence of these powerful patrons, and the municipal authorities favoured other schemes. The race course was allowed to erect new fencing which cut through the course. Instead St Andrews was booming and became the centre of the golfing world. The history of the course has recently been told by George M. Colville in his *Five Open Champions and the Musselburgh Golf Story* Musselburgh 1980.

The Course: The links are, at last, being given the attention they deserve, and there is a full-time greenkeeper. It is now an important local course for local people. It starts at the west end near the abandoned former clubhouse of the Burgess golfers. Behind the first green is the racecourse stand—site of the former clubhouse of the Honourable Company. To the right of the next three holes is the noisy, busy A1 road to England, and on to which the Musselburgh golfers sliced their shots, and played back to the links using the new brass-soled clubs. At the 4th green still stands Mrs Forman's pub but the hatch in its wall that was used to pass refreshment to the 19th-century golfers has now gone. The course turns towards the sea, and becomes less interesting. The famous Pandy bunker has been grassed over, but the racecourse fencing has been reduced and is less intrusive.

To get there: Easily found beside the racecourse on the A1 to the east of Musselburgh.

Neighbouring Courses: There is the *Musselburgh Golf Club* at Monktonhall nearby. The Edinburgh clubs are to the west, *Royal Musselburgh* is to the east, and the great golfing area at *Gullane* (39), *North Berwick* (62), *Muirfield* (57), *Kilspindie* and *Luffness* (51) is near.

60. Nairn Nairn, Nairnshire
TEL: Nairn (0667) 53208

Visitors: Freely admitted: a starting sheet is available in summer. There are many open tournaments for visitors and the long established teaching Golf Week is held each spring. There is a comfortable clubhouse.

History: The course was designed by Archie Simpson in 1887 and Braid made some modifications later. The Northern Open is played here regularly. Gregor McIntosh, one of Scotland's best known club professionals, kept a watchful eye on the links for many years.

The Course: 6483 yds SSS 71 This is one of the great championship courses of Scotland and there are fine distant views of the west coast mountains from the first tee. The tough start is usually made more difficult by having to play into the prevailing wind and the beach is a hazard on the right for five holes, although it is not out of bounds. After the 5th the gorse closes in and slack shots are cruelly punished. The huge greens are fast and true and the 14th is the most convoluted in Scotland.

There are fine views over the Cromarty Firth to the Black Isle and beyond, and oil rigs and tugs now enliven the seascape. Some parts of the course have suffered from erosion and blown sand, and a sandstorm interrupted the 1957 Northern Open. Nairn has the best putting green in Scotland, and has a spacious practice area as well as a short 9-hole course.

Best Hole: 5th— see 'Best Holes' p. 130.

To get there: Take the road to the beach on the west side of the town.

Neighbouring Courses: *Nairn Dunbar* is at the east end of the town; good courses at *Elgin* (25), *Forres, Lossiemouth* (50) and *Inverness* (42) are close.

61. Newtonmore

Newtonmore, Inverness-shire

TEL: Newtonmore (05403) 328

Visitors: Freely welcome: there are open tournaments for visitors in summer.

The Course: 5982 yds   SSS 68   The first two and last two holes are on moorland while the rest (after a fine downhill drive at the third) lie on flat land beside the River Spey, with fine views of the distant Cairngorms. The short 17th hole is much admired. There is a small, friendly clubhouse.

To get there: Signposted in the middle of Newtonmore main street.

Neighbouring Courses: There are 18 holes close by at *Kingussie* (45) overlooking the valley and a new 9-holes at Dalfaber Village *Aviemore* (2). The Kincraig and Rothiemurchus courses no longer exist but there is great golf at *Boat of Garten* (7) and *Grantown-on-Spey* (38).

Other Activities: There is fine fishing on the Spey plus tennis and bowling in the village. Pony trekking and walking are favourites of visitors here.

62. North Berwick

Beach Road, North Berwick

TEL: North Berwick (0620) 2666 (Starter)

Visitors: Freely admitted, but the course is busy in summer; there is a short course for children.

History: This is the thirteenth oldest club in the world, and is second only to St Andrews in having had continuous play on one site. Golf was played here long before the North Berwick club was formed in 1832 and it had to compete with the many other activities of the town. The course gradually extended along the beach reaching its present form in 1895 although it was not until much later that the town got ownership of the land. Like some other fine courses, it was formerly played 'backwards' in winter, to protect the links.

When the railway reached North Berwick it was successfully promoted as a fashionable holiday resort—the 'Biarritz of the North'. This was strengthened when A. J. Balfour, the golfing Prime Minister, patronised the town at the turn of the century, becoming a single figure handicap player under the tuition of Tom Dunn. Other visitors were less interested in the game and Joyce Wethered later complained that ladies golf in the season at North Berwick was simply a fashion parade. Like Musselburgh and St Andrews the town and links brought forth great professionals and club makers, notably Ben Sayers.

North Berwick is now sustained, not by the big hotels, but by caravanners. The formerly exclusive clubs of the town now make visiting golfers welcome.

The history of golf here is recorded by A. B. Adamson *In the Wind's Eye* North Berwick 1980.

The Course: 6310 yds SSS 70 These ancient links give the traditional seaside challenges to golf shot making, and the hazards include the beach (not out of bounds), walls across the links, bunkers, streams and some light rough. Two holes, the 14th (Perfection) and 15th (Redan) were copied in the construction of many other courses, notably the first championship course in America—the National Golf Links on Long Island. North Berwick has been used for the Scottish Boys championship and the World Seniors Tournament, and is in good condition throughout the year.

The putting green is kept to a high standard for the many open putting competitions held here.

Best Hole: 15th — see 'Best Holes' p. 130.

To get there: Easily found in the centre of town.

Neighbouring Courses: The *East Links* at North Berwick are adjacent, further east there is the fine course at *Dunbar* (21). *Muirfield* (57) and *Gullane* (39) are to the west.

Other Activities: The beaches here and the heated outdoor pool are popular with swimmers. Sea and loch fishing is plentiful and there are a number of nature trails.

63. Oban (Glencruitten Golf Course)
Glencruitten Road, Oban, Argyll
TEL: Oban (0631) 62868

Visitors: Welcome.

The Course: 4414 yds   SSS 63   The attractive town of Oban perches on a rocky sea-coast, and the short golf course designed by James Braid is laid out in a lush valley lined by crags. Many of the tees and greens are perched high on the sides of sculptured recesses. Some thrilling drives are called for and the second shots up out of the valley can also be difficult. There is a fine new clubhouse.

To get there: Signposted on the A816 to the south of the town.

Neighbouring Courses: There was a nine hole course at Ganavan but the nearest 18-hole course is now at *Fort William* (29) sixty miles to the north. Other courses are at *Lochgilphead* and *Machrihanish* (53) to the south.

Other Activities: Trips to the western islands are popular, as are sea and loch fishing. Pony trekking, sailing and skin diving are also well organised locally.

64. Panmure (Barry)

Barry, Angus
TEL: Carnoustie (0241) 53120

Visitors: Welcome: some restrictions.

History: The club was formed in 1845 and first played over the Monifieth Links. Because of increasing congestion there they moved north to the present site in 1899.

The splendid clubhouse was deliberately built near the railway station, and hence the start and finish of the course is over rather flat land adjacent to the true links. The club drew up one of the early codes of rules for playing golf and they were the first to introduce a rule dealing with the unplayable lie. Hogan practised secretly here before winning the Carnoustie Open Championship of 1953.

The Course: 6289 yds SSS 70 The course touches the Monifieth links at its eastern end, but it has more gorse and pines than its neighbour. The railway is a hazard, as is the Buddon burn in front of the 12th green.

Best Hole: 6th — see 'Best Holes' p. 130.

To get there: Turn south off the A930 in Barry village.

Neighbouring Courses: *Monifieth* (55) and *Carnoustie* (12).

Other Activities: See *Carnoustie*.

65. Peebles

Peebles Municipal Golf Course
Kirkland Street, Peebles
TEL : Peebles (0721) 20197 (Club)
20153 (Secretary)

Visitors: Welcome, but week-ends are busy.

The Course: 6137 yds   SSS 69   The course climbs slowly from the modernised clubhouse on to higher ground above the town. From the high points at the 4th and 7th holes there is a wide view of Peebles and district. The turf and greens have a fine quality. Players here find the last hole—the 18th—to be the most testing, as coming at the end of the round the 480 yard hole is a demanding par 5.

The course is a favourite with golfing societies and with visitors to the Hydro who run a Golf Week here in August.

To get there: Signposted at the west end of town.

Neighbouring Courses: *West Linton* is much admired as are the courses further down the Tweed— *Innerleithen* and *Galashiels*.

Other Attractions: Neidpath Castle is close to the course and the town has many leisure facilities, including fishing on the Tweed.

66. Pitlochry Pitlochry, Perthshire
TEL: Pitlochry (0796) 2792

Visitors: Welcome. There are numerous open competitions including the Highland Opens in July and August, which have both scratch and handicap sections.

The Course: 5811 yds   SSS 68   The course is of championship standards, and was laid out by W. Fernie of Troon in 1909. The clubhouse is set high above Pitlochry and the course climbs even higher. The first hole is a dramatic start to the course. It requires a drive which clears the cross bunkers near the tee. A penal bunker guards the climb to the elevated sloping green. Once on the green a new danger emerges; if it is fast, players have been known to putt off the surface. The 16th hole has fine views of the Tay and Tummel valleys. John Panton, one of Scotland's leading professionals, learnt to play the game here.

To get there: Watch for a signpost at the north end of the main street.

Neighbouring Courses: There are neat riverside 9-hole courses at *Aberfeldy, Blair Atholl* and on the moor at *Dunkeld. Taymouth Castle* is a lush, parkland 18-hole course near Kenmore.

Other Activities: Pitlochry has a full range of tourist facilities including a fine putting course, fishing, pony trekking, nature trails and a sports centre. The dam at Loch Faskally is of interest. In summer the famous Festival Theatre is an attraction.

67. Powfoot Annan, Dumfriesshire

TEL: Cummertrees (04617) 227

Visitors: Welcome.

History: The eastern part of the course was flattened during the last war for use as a camp. Thus only the west part of the course retains its links character.

The Course: 6011 yds   SSS 69   The fine links turf and gorse at the west end make for some good individual holes, where the sea is almost reached. There is a pleasant golfers' hotel at the east side of the links, and the course returns to the clubhouse at a number of points.

To get there: Turn south at Cummertrees on the B724 Annan to Dumfries road.

Neighbouring Courses: *Southerness* (73) and the two parkland courses at *Dumfries* (19).

Other Activities: This region is a major area for sea, loch and river fishing, and there are fine beaches.

68. Prestwick Golf Club
(Old Prestwick)
Links Road, Prestwick, Ayrshire
TEL: Prestwick (0292) 77404

Visitors: Welcome, but by arrangement with the Secretary.

History: The club was founded in 1851, and the members enticed Tom Morris from St Andrews to become their professional. Shortly afterwards in 1860 they announced 'A General Golf Tournament for Scotland', afterwards renamed the Open Championship, which can still claim to be the premier tournament in the world. The Open was held at Prestwick frequently thereafter, but in 1925 MacDonald Smith was mobbed during his last round, and it became clear that crowd control here was no longer possible. The Amateur Championship was last held here in 1952, but the Scottish Amateur continues to come to Prestwick.

In 1977 Henry Cotton unveiled a plaque near the clubhouse beside the 14th hole to commemorate the starting point of the original Championship course. Though this old first hole was 578 yards in length (reaching to the present 16th green) Young Tom Morris had a 3 there in one of his winning rounds of the Open.

The members are active in their support of older golfing traditions and the ancient clubhouse contains many golfing relics, photographs and engravings. There is a history of the older days of the club by James E. Shaw, *Prestwick Golf Club* Glasgow 1938.

The Course: 6544 yds   SSS 72   'A course without enemies' said Bernard Darwin. The eight holes near the clubhouse are a marvel of compact design and are justly famous. At the first hole the railway line occupies what used to be the right hand side of the fairway, and after the beautiful short 2nd, there is the Cardinal hole (505 yds), perhaps the best par 5 in the world. The second shot has to clear the huge bunker buttressed with sleepers and at the same time try to cut the corner towards the tiny green. The 4th is simple and treacherous, curving to the right round the slow turn of the burn. The penal bunker at 200 yards from the tee was inserted by James Braid. The next few holes were not part of the original course, but fit well with the ancient style. The real Prestwick links return at the edge of the 12th green, where the boundary wall formerly ran, and the 13th has one of the smallest and trickiest greens in Scottish golf.

The finishing 'loop', though modest in length, is full of hazard, and delight. It is not, therefore, in tune with modern design, but makes a thrilling finish for match play, since cunning rather than force is required to conquer these final holes. The Alps, 385 yards (17th) has its famous blind second shot to a closely bunkered green.

To get there: Easily found near the railway station in the centre of town.

Best Hole: 3rd (Cardinal) — see 'Best Holes' p. 130.

Neighbouring Courses: *Prestwick St Nicholas* and *Prestwick St Cuthbert* are close, as are the private and municipal courses at *Troon* (77, 78), *Irvine, Ayr, Gailes* (32, 80) and *Barassie* (6).

69. Reay Reay, Caithness

TEL: Reay (084781) 288

Visitors: Admitted freely: there are open tournaments in the summer.

The Course: 5875 yds   SSS 68   This course is set in classical links land beside high sandy dunes, and intelligent use of the ground and natural hazards has been made. The nuclear reactor at Dounreay is fortunately just out of sight. Even at the height of summer, the course is not crowded. The greens were saved in the droughts of 1976 by water pumped from the streams on the course. There is great local golfing rivalry with the Thurso club.

To get there: Easily found on the A386 to the east of the village.

Neighbouring Courses: To the east, there are 18 holes on the moor at *Thurso*, and the club at *Wick* (81). There is no golf to the west of Reay.

Other Activities: Loch and sea fishing is important here, and sailing and skin-diving can be had at Thurso.

70. Rosemarkie

(Fortrose and Rosemarkie)
Ness Road, Fortrose, Inverness-shire
TEL: Fortrose (0381) 20529/20733

Visitors: Welcome.

The Course: 5890 yds   SSS 69   Opened in 1888, this was one of James Braid's last courses. Laid out on sandy links beside a pebbly beach, this is a traditional course for family holiday golf. It has a simple nine-out, nine-back layout on the sandy peninsula and there is a rather sombre view of Fort George barracks from the far end of the course. During World War II, the links were used for practice sea-borne assaults, and the golf course suffered some damage.

To get there: Easily found near the town.

Neighbouring Courses: Close by are *Muir of Ord* and *Strathpeffer*. The new road bridges from the south and north to the Black Isle bring closer the courses at *Nairn* (60), *Inverness* (42), *Invergordon* and *Tain* (76). *Royal Dornoch* (17) is 60 miles away.

Other Activities: There is a fine beach and good sailing and fishing.

71. Rosemount

(Blairgowrie Golf Club)
Rosemount, Blairgowrie, Perthshire
TEL: Blairgowrie (0250) 2594/3116 (Starters Box)

Visitors: Admitted, but there are limited starting times.

History: The course was founded in 1889 by golfing enthusiasts from Dundee and the final design was by Dr Alastair Mackenzie. The popularity of the club has enabled a second full 18-hole course to be constructed around the original one. Many of the greens were destroyed by disease in 1962 and new ones were constructed.

The Course: 6700 yds SSS 72 The remarkable feature of this course is the individuality of the holes cut out of a forest of pines and birch. So isolated are the players that they may lose their sense of direction and even become apprehensive about a safe return to the clubhouse. The isolation also encourages a large variety of wild life, which can add interest to a round.

The long holes, with their wide lush fairways and large greens, favour modern target golf. The best of these holes is the 468 yard 16th. After a thrilling drive over the Black Loch, there is a shot, or a series of shots, to a narrow green set in the famous Rosemount woods. The club is regularly used for major tournaments.

To get there: Found to the south of Blairgowrie between the Perth and Coupar Angus roads.

Neighbouring Courses: *Alyth* (1), the Perth courses, *Pitlochry* (66), and the sporty course at *Glenshee*, the only 6-hole course in Scotland.

Other Attractions: There is fishing on the Dean Water and River Isla, and water ski-ing at Drumore Loch.

72. St Andrews
St Andrews, Fife
TEL: St Andrews (0334) 3393 (Old Course Starter)

History: Though it cannot be claimed with certainty that golf originated at St Andrews, the game has been played here for so long and played so seriously, that it is universally recognised as the home of golf. The town has raised more generations of professionals and club makers than elsewhere, and it was St Andrews that taught the game to Charles Macdonald, the founding father of golf in America, while he was a student here. But above all, St Andrews has the Royal and Ancient Golf Club, who have played golf on one site longer than any other club in the world, who drew up the first set of rules to be widely used, and who continue to regulate the game throughout the world.

The uneven St Andrews links, from the start, gave to the game the need for skill, while retaining an element of chance; exposure to the wind and weather of the east coast called for continual exercise of judgement and golfing cunning rather than mere calculation. Though many of the world's great players, including Bobby Jones, ultimately came to admire it unreservedly, many have been puzzled and irritated by the Old Course during their first encounter.

The lay-out here repays study. In an earlier day the course had only nine greens which were used both for the players going out and coming in (hence the names like 'High Hole Out' and 'High Hole In'). But by 1832 golf was becoming popular, the greens were expanded, and two holes were cut in each green to speed up the play. The 'in' and 'out' holes had to be distinguished and were marked with flags of different colours, a code copied slavishly elsewhere throughout the world. The original lay-out even allowed that in a former day it could be played backwards (i.e. from the 2nd tee to the 16th green etc.), a method still used in winter to protect the course. The last Open to be played on the 'backward' course was in 1886.

Of the many books on St Andrews golf, the best is probably Dawson Taylor *St Andrews—Cradle of Golf* London 1976.

The Courses: At St Andrews the golfer has many choices—four courses, a splendid putting green (the Himalayas) and a driving range.

All the golf is open to the public, though a ballot operates for busy times in summer and club competitions may occupy the tee on occasions. The **Old Course** and the **New** are of much the same length (6500 yards) but the **Eden** and **Jubilee** courses are shorter at 5900 yards. Play on the **Balgove** course for children is inexpensive.

A number of clubhouses cluster round the start of the Old Course, including the Royal and Ancient Golf Club. Sunday golf here is still forbidden, since, as Tom Morris observed, the course needed the rest, even if the golfers didn't.

The Old Course: Though some say that the New course is a better conventional test of golf than the Old Course, the ancient links are unequalled in their subtlety and magical atmosphere. To walk onto the first tee, overlooked by the houses of the town and its golf clubs, is to step nervously into the history of centuries. The hazards here were not designed but evolved. Even the last hole and the first are full of cunning yet the hazards are only a burn and a hollow at the 18th green—the Valley of Sin. Of the many tales of woe at the Swilcan Burn in front of the 1st green the most dramatic was during a 4-way play-off for the Amateur Championship in 1895, when the stroke play title went to the only player to stay out of the burn at the first extra hole. On this first tee have stood all sorts and conditions of golfers, great and small and including Captains of the R and A and bemused beginners. Yet this tee is a public place and the golfer is aware keenly that the townspeople are about their normal business, not only to left and right, but astonishingly also to the front, where a public path crosses the sacred links. From there on, the links are more subtly brutal and the small and large hidden bunkers draw in badly hit shots. The more directly the ball is hit at the flag, the more serious are the risks: once on the green there can be putts of huge length. The wind can dominate play on the course and cause havoc with judgement. The 9th and 10th holes are flat and short and perhaps lack the inspiration of the rest of the course. There have been suggestions that two holes on the adjacent New course could be substituted during major tournaments.

Coming back towards the town, the 11th hole crosses the 7th without the players noticing, and hence it may not be realised that the 7th crossed the 11th. The penal bunkers at the 12th are hidden which is excusable since they were designed for the 'backward' play of the course. Though the 14th is always the toughest hole in any championship, the 17th, coming at the end of a round is perhaps the greatest strategic hole in the world of golf: players in the 1978 Open could only average 4.82 strokes at this 461 yard hole.

Best Hole: 17th — see 'Best Holes' p. 130.

To get there: No help is required. There is a large car park and changing accommodation is now available.

Neighbouring Courses: All the Fife courses are within reach and *Leuchars, Scotscraig, Crail, Elie* (26) and *Ladybank* (46) are the closest. The Dundee and Angus courses to the north are also all reachable.

Other Activities: Many are surprised that this town also offers good beaches, bathing and skin diving. There is tennis and yachting and also some nature trails, plus theatre and festivals during the university terms.

73. Southerness
Southerness, Dumfries DG2 8AZ
TEL: Kirkbean (038788) 677

Visitors: Welcome: there are open tournaments in the summer.

History: Opened in 1947, this was the first course to be built in Scotland after World War II, and it was designed by Mackenzie Ross, creator of Turnberry. A modern clubhouse has been added to what was rather an isolated course.

The Course: 6548 yds   SSS 72   This course, spread generously over links land, has gentle humps and hollows and recessed bunkers. The greens are hard and fast, and there are fine distant views of the Solway coast. On a windy day, the challenge is magnified. Though the course is long, there are five par 3s: this means that the par 4 holes are particularly long—nine of them over 400 yards.

Best Hole: 12th — see 'Best Holes' p. 130.

To get there: Easily found beside the road to Southerness from the A710.

Neighbouring Courses: Two good parkland courses at *Dumfries* (19), two more at *Dalbeattie*, the course at *Powfoot* (67), and 9 holes at *Lochmaben*.

Other Activities: Nearby are beaches and excellent fishing, both sea and fresh water.

74. Stonehaven

Stonehaven, Kincardineshire

TEL: Stonehaven (0569) 62124

Visitors: Welcome.

The Course: 5106 yds   SSS 65   There hardly seems room for the course between the rocky cliffs and the railway line to Aberdeen, but some fine holes with great views have been laid out here. The start is towards the sea cliffs, and the second tee perches high above the beach below. The danger of losing one's golf ball forever gets less as the game goes on, and there are many attractive holes to enjoy.

The course is not long, but the North Sea winds can make play difficult.

To get there: Easily found to the north of the town.

Neighbouring Courses: The *Aberdeen* (3) courses are to the north and *Banchory* and *Auchenblae* are close by.

75. Stranraer

Creachmore, Stranraer, Wigtownshire
TEL: Leswalt (077687) 245

Visitors: Welcome: there are open touraments in the summer.

History: James Braid died shortly after laying out this course. The last hole is named in his honour and his son presented a cup in Braid's memory to the club. This is a municipal course, but on land some distance from the town, since the original course was taken over for a military camp in the last war.

The Course: 6293 yds   SSS 71   Though in south-west Scotland, the course looks north and east, such is the shape of the Rhinns of Galloway here: Ailsa Craig can be seen on a good day. The line of the trees seen across Loch Ryan from the 5th hole is of the disposition of the British troops at Corunna under Sir J. Moore. The course enjoys mild weather at all times.

To get there: Easily found on the A718 to the north of Stranraer.

Neighbouring Courses: There is a good bunkerless course on the cliffs above *Portpatrick*. The 9 holes beside the beach at the *St Medan* club (Monreith by Port William) are worth a visit, as are those at *Glenluce* (the Wigtownshire County Golf Club).

Other Activities: There are fine beaches with safe bathing and water ski-ing.

76. Tain Chapel Road, Tain, Ross-shire
TEL: Tain (0862) 2314

Visitors: Welcome, but busy at weekends: there are frequent open competitions and a famous and convivial Golf Week is held in August. A modern clubhouse has replaced the ancient sociable wooden shelter.

The Course: 6207 yds   SSS 70   These fine holes were laid out by Tom Morris in 1890, and the course still reflects his genius. Set on sandy links, the course changes direction frequently. The first five holes, though not long, are extremely difficult and the 2nd, in particular, can cause early despair. The greens are unusually fast and hard. At the 11th tee, one of the most testing on the course, there is a bench seat provided by 'The Stotters' — a convivial visitors club—and the nameplates there record former members. The 16th and 17th cross and re-cross the Tain River and the back tee at the 18th brings the water into play again. The course in many ways resembles St Andrews, even in the views of the spires and public buildings of the town.

Best Hole: 3rd (412 yds) — see 'Best Holes' p. 130.

To get there: See signposts in main street.

Neighbouring Courses: Sporty 9-hole courses are found at *Alness, Invergordon, Portmahomack* and *Bonar Bridge*. The 18 holes at the spa town of *Strathpeffer* have rejuvenating properties, on account of the gradients at the 1st and 2nd holes.

Other Activities: There are beaches locally and excellent fresh and sea water fishing. This is the oldest Royal Burgh in Scotland and there are numerous other attractions for visitors.

77. Troon – Royal Troon

Craigend Road, Troon, Ayrshire
TEL: Troon (0292) 311555

Visitors: Restricted but not discouraged: apply ahead.

History: Founded in 1878, this private club has hosted the Open Championship on a number of occasions, including 1982. The first Open here in 1923 is remembered for the last minute ban on deeply ribbed iron clubs and Hagen's protest at the exclusion of the professionals from the clubhouse. In 1950 Bobby Locke won and in 1962 Palmer mastered the parched links. By contrast, Tom Weiskopf had to overcome wind and rain in his 1973 triumph.

The club was the first in Scotland to provide water to the fairways, an innovation introduced during the droughts of the 1970s. The club was given Royal status in 1978. A second course (**Portland** 6274 yds) belongs to the club and is also a fine test of golf.

The history of the club is recorded in Ian M. Mackintosh *Troon Golf Club* Troon 1974.

The Course: 6664 yds   SSS 73   The 6th (577 yds) and the 8th (126 yds) are the longest and shortest holes in Scottish championship golf. The first three holes offer a chance to get below par and the first six and last five holes follow the gentle curve of the coastline.

From the famous 8th (Postage Stamp) onwards the holes are on uneven ground. The Postage Stamp—short but treacherous—has claimed many victims and a serious competitor in the 1950 Open took 15 strokes. Sarazen holed out in one here in the 1973 open, live on television. The railway runs close to the green of the dog-leg 11th, and in the 1962 Open only Palmer mastered this hole when the droughts made it almost impossible to hold the tee shot on the fast fairways. Nicklaus took 10 shots here in the same tournament.

The apparently innocent and bunkerless 13th hole has proved to be the most difficult to par during Open Championships and Bobby Locke picked it as one of his greatest holes in the world of golf. The last five holes are testing and can be particularly difficult into the wind. The long par 3 at the 17th threatens tournament leaders with a bogey.

Best Hole: 8th — see 'Best Holes' p. 130.

To get there: Found by the sea front in the town.

Neighbouring Courses: *Prestwick Old* (68), *Prestwick St Nicholas*, the parkland *Prestwick St Cuthbert, Barassie* (6) and the two courses at *Gailes* (32, 80).

78. Troon Municipal

Troon, Ayrshire.

TEL: Troon (0292) 312464

Visitors: Freely welcome to all these busy courses: week-end play can be booked up to one week ahead on the Darley and Lochgreen courses: on weekdays, there is a starting sheet for all three courses.

The Courses: Lochgreen 6765 yds   SSS 72; Darley 6326 yds   SSS 70; Fullarton 5064 yds   SSS 65   No other town is better supplied with municipal golf, except perhaps St Andrews. Even so, more people play here each day than anywhere else in Scotland. These three remarkable municipal courses apread out like a fan from the clubhouse (which also houses a private club) and offer a graded series of golfing challenges. **Lochgreen** is very long and being of championship standard, it is sometimes used as a qualifying course when the Open is played in Ayrshire. It is long, but fair, and the greens are small and level. The **Fullarton** course is shorter and gives an enjoyable, but less testing game of golf. The **Darley** course is intermediate in length and challenge.

To get there: Clubhouse is easily found beside the railway station.

Neighbouring Courses: *Royal Troon* (77) and its relief course, *Troon Portland* are near. The municipal courses of Ayr—*Belleisle, Seafield* and *Dalmilling* are to the south. The *Prestwick* courses (68) are also near.

Other Activities: The beach is popular and there is a race course. Fishing can be had in the River Ayr, and skin diving is well organised locally.

79. Turnberry
Turnberry Hotel, Ayrshire
TEL: Turnberry (06553) 202 (Hotel)

Visitors: Welcome, but hotel guests have preference. There is a local club of small membership which plays over the courses.

History: The original hotel course was taken over during the last war to make an airfield, but the courses were reconstructed afterwards to a design by MacKenzie Ross. The remains of the old runways now provide extensive car parking space during big tournaments.

The course was changed a little for its first Open Championship in 1977. New bunkers and tees were added, together with a change in the last hole to create the dog-leg fairway. A new small clubhouse was also constructed then for the first time. A helicopter landing pad is available.

The Courses: Ailsa (Championship) 6370 yds   SSS 71 (longer for tournaments); Arran 6350 yds   SSS 70   The Championship course was at 6875 yards for the 1977 Open, but it can be even longer. Par 4 holes of increasing length lead to the short 4th with its high well-protected green perched above the rough and the beach. Four more holes along the dunes include a par 3 of around 220 yards. The tee at the 9th, placed on a rocky promontory, above the Firth of Clyde and backed by an elegant lighthouse, is much photographed. Natural hazards make the short 15th difficult and the improved 18th finishes beside the new clubhouse.

The wind here is occasionally fierce and can dominate the golf, particularly in autumn, as some tournament organisers know to their cost. The relief Arran course has flatter contours and lusher turf; it is only slightly shorter than the big course when played off the usual tees.

To get there: Easily found on the A719 coast road from Girvan to Ayr via Maidens.

Neighbouring Courses: *Girvan's* links (31) to the south and *Maybole's* 9 holes are near: to the north are all the famous Ayrshire links, and there is splendid golf at *Troon* (77 and 78) and *Ayr*.

Other Activities: Beautiful beaches are found locally, with sailing and fishing available.

80. Western Gailes
Gailes, by Irvine, Ayrshire
TEL: Irvine (0294) 311357

Visitors: By arrangement with Secretary.

History: This was a course built for Glasgow merchants on uneven ground beside the railway line and nearer to the sea than their neighbour at Glasgow Gailes. The club was host to the Curtis Cup in 1974, and thus allowed women into the clubhouse for the first time.

The Course: 6763 yds   SSS 72   A new road in connection with the development of Irvine meant that the northern part of the course was redesigned and the changes which created a new 3rd, 4th and 5th holes were welcomed. The short 5th with its blind drive was thus removed. The course is set in fine natural links and the 2nd and 6th are classic seaside holes. There is a clubhouse which maintains the old traditions of service.

To get there: Turn off the Irvine to Ayr road at the Gailes road-end and cross the railway by the new automatic level crossing, which replaced the manually operated gates.

Neighbouring Courses: *Glasgow Gailes* (32), *Irvine Bogside* and *Barassie* (6).

81. Wick Reiss, Wick, Caithness
TEL: Wick (0955) 2726

Visitors: Welcome.

The Course: 5931 yds   SSS 69   The course is set in the humps and hollows behind the dunes of Sinclair's Bay, but the magnificent seascape is only seen at the start and finish. Strictly nine out to the River Wester and nine back, the fairways are kindly, and the bunkers few. The famous Caithness winds often make scoring difficult.

To get there: Easily found at Reiss, three miles north of Wick on the A9 road to John o'Groats.

Neighbouring Courses: *Reay* (69), *Thurso*, are to the north and the 9-hole course at *Lybster*, one of the shortest in Scotland, is to the south.

Other Activities: There is a fine swimming pool, and sea angling and sailing are particularly good.

The best holes
in Scottish Golf

A great golf hole lingers in the mind long after it has been played and it is anticipated long before it is reached again. The flight of the ball is watched with unusual anxiety, and a par or better gained gives a warm glow of satisfaction.

In making this personal selection of the best holes in Scotland I have made four lists, one from the links courses and one from the parkland clubs. Many memorable holes in Scotland defy fitting into any of these categories, these are put together as a 'Sporty Nine' and a 'Scenic Nine'.

Only one hole from each course has been chosen in each section.

The Best Links Holes

The low links land round the Scottish coast nurtured the game of golf from its infancy. It is from these courses that this selection is made, and it is a tradition that the Open Championships are only played on such courses. In choosing such an imaginary round of 18 holes from these great Scottish links it is inevitable that many fine holes have to be omitted. But no-one would disagree that all the holes in this eclectic card are of the finest quality.

		Yds	par
Machrihanish	1st	423	4
Montrose	3rd	156	3
Dornoch	4th	417	4
Troon	8th	126	3
Murcar	7th	410	4
Panmure	6th	386	4
Southerness	12th	419	4
Nairn	5th	379	4
Muirfield	9th	495	5
	Out	3211	35

		Yds	par
Tain	3rd	439	4
Balgownie	9th	455	4
Prestwick	3rd	505	5
North Berwick	15th	192	3
Buckie Strathlene	17th	379	4
Carnoustie	17th	438	4
Cruden Bay	8th	225	3
St Andrews	17th	466	4
Lossiemouth	18th	423	4
	In	3552	35
	Out	3211	35
		6763	70

Machrihanish 1st (423 yds)

This hole is a great start to our collection and is a tough start to this fine course. It is perhaps the most testing opening shot in Scottish golf, and one enjoyed by those watching and waiting to play. The golfer has to compute the effects of the weather and wind, the tee in use, his or her health and strength, and then hit out boldly to the left over the Atlantic beach (which is not out of bounds) to land on the obliquely-running fairway. The alternative is to play safe to the right and accept a bogey. The huge green, when reached, is kindly and ingathering.

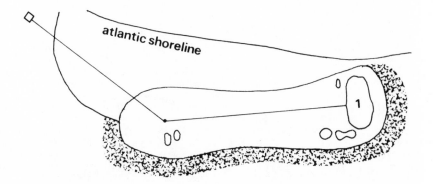

Montrose 3rd (156 yds)

This should be an easily reachable short hole, but is a testing one dominated by the ever-present wind's strength and direction. The problem is to hold the ball on a green which is generously wide but not deep. If the ball falls short it ends in a deep grassy chasm from which recovery on to the unseen green above is a gamble: there are also similar troubles behind the green.

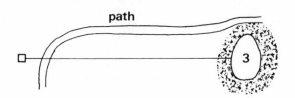

Dornoch 4th (417 yds)

Donald Ross's design at its best in this peaceful yet renowned course in the north. A diagonal drive on to a hump-backed fairway is followed by a long shot on to a huge raised green, protected in front by a trough, and on which three putts are not a disgrace.

To the right of the fairway the ball can run into a unique and unpleasant hazard—a series of small, deep, steep-walled, grassy valleys—from which a long shot on to the green is not possible.

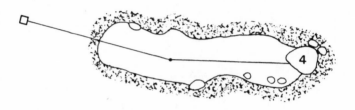

Royal Troon 8th (The Postage Stamp—126 yds)

Certainly the shortest and best known of the par 3 Open Championship holes. Once the ball is on the green, there are no problems: getting it there poses difficulties. From off the green the recovery shots from the small bunkers, valleys and mounds demand great skill. Sarazen holed in one here in 1973, but in the 1950 Open, a serious German entrant took 15.

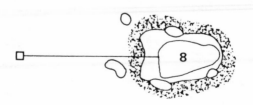

Murcar 7th (410 yds)

Archie Simpson, the designer of Murcar, considered this to be one of his best holes. There is, on the left, a safe, longer line to the green and a shorter dangerous one to the right: a tightly bunkered green completes this famous hole.

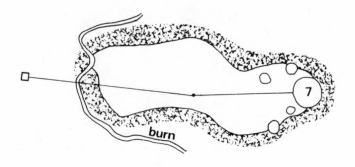

Panmure 6th (386 yds)

The drive requires a long carry and is followed by a tricky shot up the narrowing fairway to a plateau green, placed perilously close to the railway line to Carnoustie.

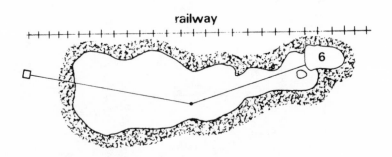

Southerness 12th (419 yds)

A great hole from this quiet and famous Mackenzie Ross course on the edge of the Solway Firth. A safe drive to the left avoids the bunkers on the right at 200 yards but lengthens the hole. The second shot to the green is usually straight into the prevailing wind and the narrow entrance to the green is flanked by a mound and a bunker.

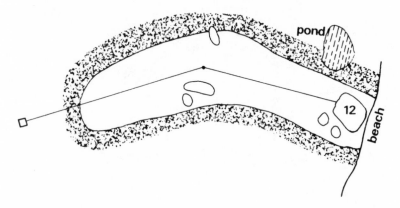

Nairn 5th (379 yds)

One of the more reachable par 4 holes on this great Moray Firth course, but a deceptive and demanding one, requiring skill rather than force. The beach to the right is not out of bounds, but the plantation to the left is. The closely guarded green is subtly elevated on the links and a second shot often falls short, since the wrong club is taken.

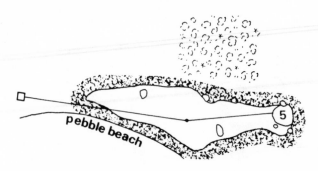

134

Muirfield 9th (495 yds)

Though a par 5 hole, this is a difficult one to finish the first half of our best 18 holes and a crucial one during Open Championships. As in many great holes there is a choice of line from the tee. The more safely the drive is played—i.e. short or to the right—the more difficult becomes the approach to the green, and the unobtrusive wall and out-of-bounds to the left become menacing. Yet the second shot must be towards this trouble, since dangerous and unseen small bunkers to the right and Simpson's bunker are on the line to the green.

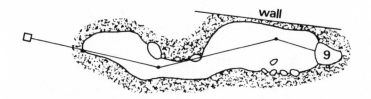

Tain 3rd (439 yds)

This is part of the wickedly difficult, but not long, start to the Tain links on the Dornoch Firth. Even if the golfer has survived the perils at the second hole, the player faces a difficult drive to the 3rd which must gain height and hold on a plateau fairway sloping left to right and also turning left. The green has a fast, deceptive surface and the approach to it is protected by an unseen, deep valley and a tiny penal bunker.

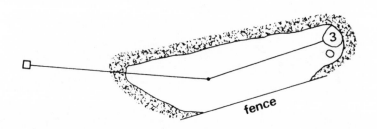

Balgownie 9th (455yds)

Another great hole from a north-east links designed by Robert Simpson. It presents, in a simple and elegant form, the classic golfing challenge—a hole turning to the right, but sloping right to left and then uphill for the second shot. Those who have suffered here should reflect that this hole is even more difficult for left-handers or habitual hookers.

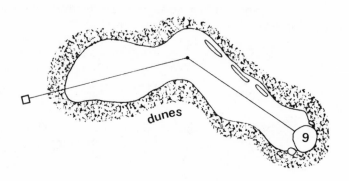

Prestwick 3rd (The Cardinal—505 yds)

One of the oldest and most respected par 5 holes in the world of golf. The tee shot sets up the second shot, which must be played perfectly and diagonally over the famous and intimidating Cardinal bunker, faced with railway sleepers. A well-played ball runs to the right leaving a short third shot to the tiny green.

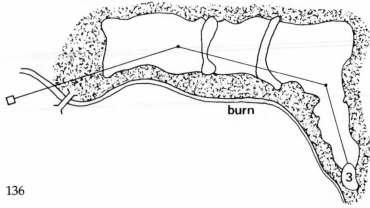

North Berwick 15th (Redan—192 yds)

Though this short hole has been widely copied by golf architects throughout the world, the hole often disappoints when first seen, since it calls for a full shot to an unseen green. At its most challenging, the pin is placed at the front of the hidden green which also slopes away from the player. Placing the pin on the left also tucks it behind a deep bunker cutting into the green. Thus even a sensible tee shot may mean a very long putt, or two, or three back.

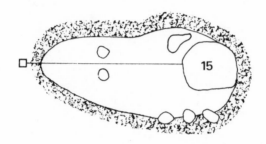

Buckie Strathlene 17th (379 yds)

After a thrilling downhill drive, the hole continues downwards and to the left beside rough ground and the cliff to the beach. The green is small, tilts to the right, and is protected by an unobtrusive ditch not in view from the fairway. Some of the perils round the green have been abolished but it is a testing hole at a crucial point in a round at Buckie.

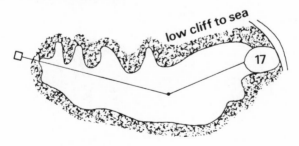

F

Carnoustie 17th (438 yds)

A great tactical hole which dominates the finish of the Open Championship when held here. A drive which is too long or too short finishes in the burn. A safe drive should land in the right hand part of the island formed by the loop of the Barry Burn. A more dangerous line is to the left, where the loop of the burn can be carried using brute force, good luck or a following wind. To attempt to carry this second loop from the back tee is foolish, and should only be attempted if you need a birdie here to win a trophy.

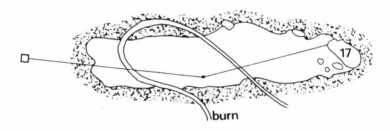

burn

Cruden Bay 8th (225 yds)

Simpson, the designer, considered this deceptively simple hole to be amongst his best. Though bunkerless, a central ridge runs on the line from tee to green, and because the hole requires a full shot, the ridge pushes a short or off line shot to the left or right into deep grassy hollows. This device was perhaps inspired by the design at Dornoch.

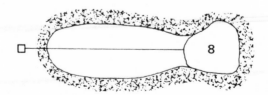

St Andrews 17th (Road Hole—466 yds)

Perhaps the best known hole in all golf and it comes at a dramatic point in the round. The drive should be sent deliberately out over the out-of-bounds on the right—formerly the railway sheds—but now the forecourt of the Old Course Hotel. The second shot is best played short and to the right, deliberately risking a bogey 5. An over-strong second shot to the narrow green risks having to play back from the road beyond, and possibly landing in the small famous bunker in front of the green, which can catch a second shot also. In this pot bunker there is hardly room for the golfer to take a stance and the pin, when in the medal position, is very close This claustrophobia, plus the genuine fear of hitting the ball back on to the road beyond the flag, has shattered the nerve of even the greatest.

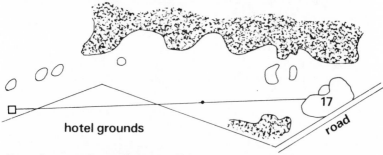

Lossiemouth 18th (423 yds)

Surely the noblest finishing hole in Scotland. The drive is along a valley overlooked by the gracious Stotfield houses with the Moray Firth and dunes to the left. The second shot must gain some height to reach the plateau green set in a natural amphitheatre in front of the solid clubhouse. The green is also beside the main street, and hence a small, well-informed audience is usually present to watch attempts at this difficult second shot.

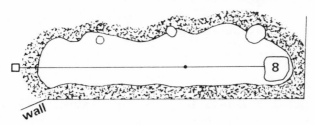

Best Inland Holes

Though Scotland's reputation comes from her links courses, a fine card can easily be chosen from the parkland courses. In making this personal selection, only one hole from each course has been chosen, and many fine holes have had to be omitted.

		Yds	par
Cardross	1st	340	4
Dalmahoy	7th	430	4
Fort William	1st	287	4
Kirriemuir	17th	200	3
Rosemount	16th	468	4
Forfar	15th	375	4
Kilmacolm	3rd	360	4
Gleddoch House	2nd	181	3
Killermont	5th	530	5
	Out	3171	35
		Yds	par
Grantown-on-Spey	12th	410	4
Elgin	5th	485	5
Pollok	17th	150	3
Boat of Garten	6th	380	4
Pitlochry	1st	398	4
Ranfurly Castle	5th	170	3
Dougalston	2nd	360	4
Lanark	1st	368	4
Gleneagles (Kings)	17th	390	4
	In	3094	35
	Out	3171	35
		6265	70

Descriptions of these holes are given with the entry for each club.

The Sporty Nine

The holes chosen above offer conventional challenges. But golf in Scotland does not always fit into such moulds and nine of the most enjoyable holes in Scotland must also be mentioned. They come from courses that might otherwise be missed and are known only to the most serious students of golf. But they are essential in describing and understanding fully the game in Scotland.

Strathpeffer Spa 1st (301 yds)

The drive from the clubhouse has the longest drop to the green from any tee in Scottish golf. The climb back up to the second green may be responsible for the well-known therapeutic properties of this spa town. Many locals start their round at the 3rd, and kindly souls in the clubhouse often suggest this to visitors.

Musselburgh 4th (Mrs Forman's—500 yds)

Once the most famous hole in Scotland, when Musselburgh was the centre of Scottish golf in the mid-nineteenth century. The course is now rather neglected but this hole still has the fairway which leads to a green without a flag. This is backed by the tavern in which Old Tom Morris had to hide, during a famous match, from the partisan supporters of Old Willie Park. In a former day, a hatch on the wall of the pub was used to serve the players.

St Medan (Port William) 4th

A splendid one-shot hole when there is no wind, and an even better one when it is blowing. From a high tee the ball has to carry down to a green with a raised apron supported by railway sleepers. A beautiful view and a sandy cove complete the delight of this fine hole.

Stonehaven 2nd (203 yds)

Not a hole for those afraid of heights: the 500 ft drop on each side of the tee encourages a nervous twitch. No immediate recovery of a loosely hit ball is possible.

Killin 9th (500 yds)

This last hole of the sporty Killin nine is a great romp downhill through mature woods with the Bridge of Lochay and the valley beyond always in view.

Blackwaterfoot 3rd (140 yds)

The tee shot at this short hole has to reach up to the unseen green perched high in a cliff. As at all blind holes here the unique Blackwaterfoot signalling system is used to indicate when the green in clear.

Carradale 7th (240 yds)

A thrilling one-shot hole requiring a long downhill drive played over moorland. The old wall guarding the green has, alas, been removed, but the village of Portrigh is still at the back.

Stornoway 1st (341 yds)

A tricky par 4 hole at the start of this well-designed parkland course. A notice on the first tee properly warns the player that the hole has a right-angled bend, unique in Scotland, at the point reached by the drive.

New Galloway 9th (345 yds)

A thrilling last hole to finish this compact moorland and tree-lined course. The drive downhill must be hit on to the only safe patch of green fairway below, and a poor tee shot will catch gorse, rough or find the trees. The second shot is similar to the first and has again to clear troublesome rough and gorse to fall neatly on to the green flanked by one of the few traditional Victorian clubhouses surviving in Scotland.

The Scenic Nine

Lastly, it must be said that there are many beautiful courses in Scotland which it has not been possible to include in the main selection. Some holes from these courses have such memorable views that they deserve a special mention.

Blairmore and Strone 7th

The height of this hole on the mountains above the Holy Loch gives a remarkable vista of the Firth of Clyde: it is not a course for those with weak hearts. The views here are rivalled only by the panorama from the 2nd hole at the Innellan course a little to the south.

Dollar 5th

A comfortable view of the gracious town of Dollar is obtained from this bunkerless course perched on the side of the Ochil Hills. Beyond are the flat lands of Clackmannan and there is a hint of the Firth of Forth in the distance.

Royal Tarlair (Banff) 13th

A short hole on the Moray Firth with a green placed high on a rocky promontory above the beach. The hole is reminiscent of Pebble Beach: perhaps Pebble Beach copied Banff.

Rothesay 12th

A tricky hole remarkably endowed with panoramic views in many directions — the Firth of Clyde and Ayrshire to the east, the Kyles of Bute and the Argyll hills to the north.

Craigie Hill (Perth) 13th

Every house and street in Perth seem visible from this tee, as are the Sidlaw Hills to the east and the Grampians to the north.

Murrayfield 2nd

Splendid distant views of Edinburgh, the Braids and the Pentland Hills are obtained from this course on the edge of the city. To the north is the Firth of Forth.

Colvend 3rd

The top of this short, friendly course perched on a promontory beside the Solway Firth, gives an interesting view of the wooded hills and villages nearby. On good days there is a long sight of the Lake District over the water.

Tobermory (any hole)

Placed high above the lovely steep-walled harbour of the town, the entire course has a breathtaking view back down the Sound of Mull to the mountains of Lorne on the mainland beyond.

Stromness 9th

From this vantage point on the course, there is an ever changing seascape to the south, where the turbulent Sound of Hoy and a lighthouse are backed by the mountains of the island of Hoy.

Gazetteer

This is a complete guide to golf in the regions of Scotland. Every course is mentioned and those areas which are not well represented in the main selection are discussed here in greater detail. Visitors are welcome at many of these courses but others, notably near major towns, are private clubs and visitors should enquire ahead regarding regulations for play. The numbers in brackets after the name of a course refer to a seperate entry in the main course guide.

Dumfries and Galloway

Those who regularly enjoy their golf in the south-west of Scotland have agreed not to tell anyone else. Golfers from England race up the A74 on their holidays to reach the Lowlands and coastal links of Scotland and Scottish holiday-makers head anywhere but south. True, the attractions of golf at **Southerness** (73), **Dumfries** (19), **Stranraer** (75) and **Moffat** (54) are well known , but those who know the classic 4th at **Port William** with its sleepered bunker by the sea and know of the thrilling finish at **New Galloway** keep their secret to themselves. These sporty courses are set in moorland above the towns as at **Dalbeattie** and **Kirkcudbright** and there are sensible 9-holes at **Lochmaben, Castle Douglas, Gatehouse of Fleet** and **Wigtown**. At Glenluce are the uncompromising links lay-out of the **Wigtownshire County Club,** now 18 holes and much improved by tree planting and there is a fine bunkerless course at **Portpatrick.** But at **Colvend** the nine holes are unique — a mountainous moorland course on the edge of the sea.

Castle Douglas
Colvend, Dalbeattie
Crichton Royal, Dumfries
Dalbeattie
Dumfries & County (19)
Dumfries & Galloway (19)
Gatehouse of Fleet
Kirkcudbright
Langholm
Lochmaben
Lockerbie

Moffat (54)
New Galloway
Portpatrick (Dunskey)
Powfoot, Annan
St. Medan, Port William
Sanquhar
Southerness (73)
Stranraer (75)
Thornhill
Wigtown & Bladnoch
Wigtownshire County
    (Glenluce)

Ayrshire

On the Ayrshire coast is found the greatest density of golf courses anywhere in Scotland. Though they are more separated from each other in the north at **Largs** and **Skelmorlie,** and also in the south at **Girvan** (31) and **Turnberry** (79), the area round Troon has about fifteen courses almost touching one another. The Open Championship was inaugurated at Prestwick and this famous competition continues to be held at **Turnberry** and **Royal Troon** (77). Here golf has had to share the flat links land with the railway and more recently, the air fields, both of which add diversions to the game.

There is a great tradition of democratic golf in this area and the three municipal links at **Troon** (78) must be the busiest single area of golf in Scotland. Lastly, the mild winters of the Ayrshire coast have made this area attractive to the golfers of Glasgow and Kilmarnock who established private clubs at **Gailes** (32 and 80) and **Barassie** (6) to enable them to play the game throughout the year.

Annanhill, Kilmarnock
Ardeer, Stevenston
Ayr, Belleisle
Ayr, Seafield
Ballochmyle, Mauchline
Barassie, (6) Troon
Beith
Caprington, Kilmarnock
Dalmilling, Ayr
Girvan (31)
Glasgow Gailes (32)
Irvine
Irvine Ravenspark
Kilbirnie Place
Largs
Largs, Routenburn
Loudoun, Galston

Maybole
New Cumnock
Prestwick (Old Prestwick) (68)
Prestwick, St. Cuthbert
Prestwick, St. Nicholas
Royal Troon (77)
    — Old Course
    — Portland Course
Skelmorlie
Troon Municipal (78) —
    Lochgreen Course
    Darley Course
    Fullarton Course
Turnberry (79) — Arran Course
                 — Ailsa Course
West Kilbride
Western Gailes (80)

The Borders

Though, in 1632, the death at Kelso of 'T Catto killed by a golf ball' is recorded, golf has never been played with the same passion in the Borders as in the rest of Scotland; but it has become increasingly popular recently.

Perhaps the sporting urges here were met instead by the Borderer's passion for rugby. Certainly the rugby pitch has pride of place in these towns, set in the flat land of the narrow valleys; and even a cricket pitch is often to be found nearby. Borders golf courses were banished to the steep hillsides around the towns, giving demanding exercise and sporty golf.

Langholm's 9 holes hug the hillside and there is still a splendid corrugated iron Victorian clubhouse. **Hawick's** (40) course is gentle at the start; whereas **Selkirk's** well designed 9 holes perch on the slopes, but give fine views of the Borders in all directions. There are scenic courses at **Peebles** (65) and **West Linton** and nine holes at **Minto, Melrose** and **St Boswells** which are not too demanding. But the **Ladhope** course at Galashiels is built on a steep hillside and gives good exercise; nearby are the 9 gentler holes at **Torwoodlee,** known locally as the Garden of Eden.

Duns
Eyemouth
Galashiels (Ladhope)
Hawick (40)
Hirsel, Coldstream
Innerleithen
Jedburgh
Kelso
Lauder

Melrose
Minto, Hawick
Newcastleton
Peebles (65)
St. Boswells
Selkirk
Torwoodlee, Galashiels
West Linton

Edinburgh and the Lothians

Few go to Edinburgh simply for a golfing holiday, but many visitors may wish to play golf. This can be difficult if no plans are made ahead. The best known courses and clubs like **Barnton (the Royal Burgess Golfing Society)** (23), **Bruntsfield Links Golfing Society** and **Murrayfield** require the visitor to play with a member or at least require advance notice and an introduction from their home club. At **Muirfield** (57) in particular, no last minute arrangements can result in entry to the sacred links, even if you have won the Open, or intend to.

In the city of Edinburgh the following clubs are hospitable at quiet times: **Silverknowes, Portobello, Liberton, Craigmillar Park, Kingsknowe, Duddingston, Prestonfield, Mortonhall** and **Torphin Hill.** Fine golf can be had at the **Braid Hills** (24) municipal courses. Out of town to the east, **Gullane** (39), **North Berwick** (62) and **Kilspindie** by the sea and the gracious courses at **Longniddry** are well worth visiting and are more open to visitors. To the west, the new country clubs at **Livingston** and **Polkemmet** have maturing courses and new clubhouses and there are attractive parkland courses at **Dalmahoy** (16) and **Ratho Park.**

Those interested in the history of the game should visit the tidy grassy park at Leith where golf was first recorded in Scotland in 1554 and they should also inspect **Bruntsfield Links**, first home of the early golf clubs. The Golf Tavern, which housed and entertained the old clubs playing over Bruntsfield Links is still there, and the links are used for pitch and putt golf by local veterans. Summer visitors can now hire old clubs and balls for a game over this short hole course. The Bruntsfield Links Golfing Society, who used the links in the 1800s and then moved out to Davidson's Mains, still return bi-ennially to play (and lose) at pitch and putt against the local experts, as do the Royal Burgess golfers.

The ancient and neglected course at **Musselburgh** (59) is also worth a visit, since it is one of the great places in golf history. The lay-out has hardly changed since the Open Championship was last played there, and golf of 19th century type is still available. Some days a green fee is collected; on others, golf is free.

Baberton, Edinburgh
Bathgate
Braid Hills (24), Edinburgh
Broomieknowe
Bruntsfield Links, Edinburgh
Carrick Knowe, Edinburgh
Craigentinny, Edinburgh
Craigmillar, Edinburgh
Dalmahoy (16)
Duddingston, Edinburgh
Dunbar (21)
Gifford
Glencorse, Penicuik
Greenburn, Fauldhouse
Gullane (39)
Haddington
Harburn, West Calder
Kilspindie
Kingsknowe, Edinburgh
Liberton, Edinburgh
Linlithgow
Livingston
Longniddry
Lothianburn, Edinburgh
Luffness New, Aberlady
Merchants of Edinburgh

Mortonhall, Edinburgh
Muirfield (57), Gullane,
   (Honourable Company of
   Edinburgh Golfers)
Murrayfield, Edinburgh
Musselburgh (59)
Newbattle, Dalkeith
North Berwick (62)
   — West Links
   — East Links
Portobello, Edinburgh
Prestonfield, Edinburgh
Pumpherston
Ratho Park, Edinburgh
Ravelston, Edinburgh
Royal Burgess (Barnton) (23),
   Edinburgh
Royal Musselburgh,
   Prestonpans
Silverknowes, Edinburgh
Swanston, Edinburgh
Torphin Hill, Edinburgh
Turnhouse, Edinburgh
Uphall
West Lothian, Bo'ness
Winterfield, Dunbar

Glasgow and Clydeside

Though the city of Glasgow is not Scotland's greatest tourist attraction, it has many virtues, among which are a large number of first-class golf courses. In such a large city these clubs cannot be as hospitable as they might otherwise wish to be, but if a visitor applies ahead, a game can usually be arranged.

Glasgow's ancient golfing area, the Glasgow Green, is no longer used for that purpose, since **The Glasgow Golf Club (Killermont)** (35) who formed their club in 1787, were forced to leave this busy common land in mid-18th century and, after a number of moves, settled at their fine course at Killermont. Another course also set in the parkland of a former stately home is **Pollok.** Further out of town are **Douglas Park, Hilton Park, Milngavie, Whitecraigs** and **Williamwood** and the extra travel to **Bonnyton, Erskine, Kilmacolm** (44), **Bridge of Weir** (8), **East Renfrewshire, Buchanan Castle** (33), and the country club at Gleddoch House, **Langbank** (48) is rewarding. **Dougalston** (34) is certainly the best course which welcomes visitors in this areas and **Cardross** (11) is also within reach.

Glasgow is also notable for its generous provision of municipal golf at cheap rates. While some of the most basic golf in the world is played on the municipal pitch-and-putt courses, there are also well laid out and testing courses, such as **Littlehill** and **Lethamhill.** Good golf is also on offer in and around Paisley and on the new course at **Renfrew.**

Alexandra Park, Glasgow	Cambuslang
Barshaw, Paisley	Cardross (11), Dumbarton
Bearsden	Cathcart Castle, Glasgow
Bishopbriggs, Glasgow	Cochrane Castle, Johnstone
Blairbeth, Rutherglen	Cathkin Braes, Rutherglen
Bonnyton, Eaglesham	Cawdor, Glasgow
Buchanan Castle (33), Drymen	Clober, Milngavie
Calderbraes, Uddingston	Clydebank & District
Caldwell	(Hardgate)

Clydebank Overtoun,
  (Dalmuir)
Crow Wood, Glasgow
Cowglen, Glasgow
Deaconsbank, Glasgow
Douglas Park, Bearsden
Dougalston (33), Milngavie
Dullatur
Dumbarton
East Kilbride
East Renfrewshire,
  Newton Mearns
Eastwood, Newton Mearns
Elderslie
Erskine
Ferenze, Barrhead
Glasgow Killermont (34)
Gleddoch House,
  Langbank (34)
Gourock
Greenock
Haggs Castle, Glasgow
Hayston, Kirkintilloch
Helensburgh
Hilton Park, Milngavie
Kilmacolm (44)
Kilsyth Lennox
Kings Park, Glasgow

Kirkhill, Cambuslang
Kirkintilloch
Knightswood, Glasgow
Lenzie
Lethamhill, Glasgow
Linn Park, Glasgow
Littlehill, Glasgow
Lochwinnoch
Mount Ellen, Glasgow
Milngavie
Paisley (Braehead)
Palacerigg, Cumbernauld
Pollok, Glasgow
Port Glasgow
Ralston, Paisley
Old Ranfurly,
  Bridge of Weir (8)
Ranfurly Castle,
  Bridge of Weir
Renfrew
Ruchill, Glasgow
Sandyhill, Glasgow
Torrance House, East Kilbride
Vale of Leven, Alexandria
Whitecraigs, Glasgow
Williamwood, Glasgow
Windyhill, Bearsden

Arran, Bute, the Cumbraes and Argyll

Golf on the islands of the Clyde coast breaks all the rules. The courses run across roads, the holes pass over ravines and cross each other. There are many courses with square greens, a few with round greens and some have no greens. There are courses with no rough and others with no fairways: there are even 12-hole courses and 13-hole courses. These eccentricities only prove that golf is played here entirely for pleasure. The final blessing is that the mild Gulf Stream round this coast ensures golf throughout the year.

Membership of all seven courses on Arran can cost less than at one on the mainland. The **Lamlash** (4681 yds) course is high above the Clyde, but **Brodick's** (4816 yds) course is beneath Goat Fell on links land beside the beach. **Lochranza** and **Machrie Bay** have 9 holes of simple construction. **Corrie** has 9 holes backed by Alpine scenery and a tiny perfect Victorian clubhouse. **Whiting Bay's** sporty course has its famous 'wall of death' at the 17th and great views of the Holy Isle and the mountains. But above all, **Blackwaterfoot** (Shiskine Golf Club) draws the holiday golfer and family. The 12-hole course is just the right length for a morning's family golf: 6 more holes were built, but no one used them. These kindly links have a unique collection of signalling devices to tell you when the hidden greens are clear.

On Bute, the **Rothesay** course (5358 yds) is flourishing and has splendid golf and views of the Firth of Clyde. If you play in the medal at **Port Bannatyne's** 13-hole course, the first five are played twice. In Bute, if you want peace to play or practice on a fine natural links course, go to **Kingarth's** 9 holes, put your money into the honesty box and enjoy the golf and the view of Arran.

There are also sporty 18-holes round the reservoir at **Millport** (5831 yds). On the mainland is the excellent course at **Dunoon** (22) and the neighbouring courses at **Blairmore and Strone** and at **Innellan** have spectacular views of the Clyde Coast. The **Kyles of Bute Golf Club** is on the moor beside Tighnabruaich, and visitors should pay into the honesty box.

Further south, the Kintyre peninsula is endowed with championship golf at **Machrihanish** (53), the well-known course at **Dunaverty** (Southend) (20), and the sporty nine holes at **Carradale** (13) and **Tarbert.**

Visitors are admitted freely at most times to all these courses but some may be busy in summer when many holiday tournaments are held.

Blairmore & Strone,
  by Dunoon
Blackwaterfoot (Shiskine),
  Arran
Brodick, Arran
Carradale (13)
Corrie, Arran
Dunaverty, Southend
Dunoon (Cowal)
Innellan, by Dunoon
Kyles of Bute, Tighnabruaich
Kingarth, Bute

Lamlash, Arran
Lochranza, Arran
Machrie Bay, Arran
Machrihanish (53),
  by Campbeltown
Millport, Cumbrae
Port Bannatyne, Bute
Rothesay
Tarbert, Argyll
Whiting Bay, Arran

Central Scotland

The position of the central belt of Scotland, between the ancient golfing areas of Ayrshire and the golfing mecca of Fife, might suggest that it has less good golf to offer. This is not so; the game has been recorded from ancient times at **Stirling** and **Lanark** (47), and the quality of the golf at **Falkirk** and **Glenbervie** is well known as it is at **Dullatur**. **Linlithgow** has some fine holes, and the high position of the **Grangemouth** course gives views of the Forth that cannot be bettered. From **Alloa** there are splendid views of the Ochil Hills on whose slopes can be found a line of sporty courses — **Bridge of Allan, Alva, Tillicoultry, Dollar** and **Muckhart**. Lastly, the area near the Clyde south of Glasgow should not be forgotten. **Drumpellier** and **East Kilbride** have mature courses and those at **Hamilton** and **Bothwell Castle** are highly regarded. Further south, at **Leadhills,** is Britain's highest course.

Airdrie	Falkirk
Alloa	Falkirk Tryst, Larbert
Alva	Glenbervie, Larbert
Balmore	Grangemouth, Falkirk
Bellshill	Hamilton
Biggar	Hamilton Municipal
Bonnybridge	Hollandbush, Lesmahagow
Bothwell Castle	Lanark (47)
Braehead, Alloa	Larkhall
Bridge of Allan	Leadhills, Biggar
Campsie, Lennoxtown	Muckhart
Carluke	Polmont, Maddiston
Carnwath	Shotts (Blairhead)
Coatbridge	Stirling
Colville Park, Motherwell	Strathaven
Dollar	Strathendrick, Drymen
Douglas Water, Rigside	Tillicoultry
Drumpellier, Coatbridge	Tulliallan
Dullatur	Wishaw
Easter Moffat, Airdrie	

Fife

St. Andrews is deservedly known as the home of golf, but it should not be forgotten that the rest of Fife has a remarkably rich range of courses to offer. There are even gracious parkland courses like **Kirkcaldy** (Dunnikier Park) but the greatest asset is the line of natural links round the coast starting at **Scotscraig** near the Tay Bridge and ending at **Aberdour** near the Forth Road Bridge. Between these two courses are the ancient links at **Leven** (49), and **Crail** plus the much admired **Elie** (26), and **Lundin Links** courses. The fame of **St. Andrews** (72), should not conceal the merits of **Ladybank** (46) nearby.

Aberdour
Anstruther
Auchterderran
Bishopshire, Kinnesswood
Burntisland House
Canmore, Dunfermline
Crail
Cupar
Dunfermline (Pitfirrane)
Elie (26)
Falkland
Green Hotel, Kinross
Glenrothes
Kinghorn
Kirkcaldy
Kirkcaldy (Dunnikier Park)
Ladybank (46)

Leslie
Leven (49) — Links
          — Scoonie
Lochgelly
Lundin Links
Milnathort
Pitreavie, Dunfermline
St. Andrews (72)
    — Old Course
    — New Course
    — Eden Course
    — Jubilee Course
    — Balgove Course
St. Michael's, Leuchars
Saline
Scotscraig, Tayport
Thornton

Perthshire

Perth, on the upper Tay estuary, was once capital of Scotland. It is one of the ancient sites of Scottish golf, since the river made it an east coast port for trade with Holland. The South Inch was probably used as the early golf links here, but extensions to the area of the North Inch made it more favoured than the South Inch in the nineteenth century. The venerable **Royal Perth Golfing Society,** founded in 1824, is still found in the town in conjunction with a County Club and it has occasional competitions over the public links. It can claim to be the oldest of the 'Royal' golf clubs, an honour occasionally disputed by Royal Musselburgh. The **Perth Artisans Club** founded in 1879 claims to be the oldest club of this kind in the world, and plays over the North Inch.

The ancient course on the **North Inch** is laid out on a flat river bed which, like the South Inch, has also been used since earliest days as common land for recreation and grazing by the people of Perth. The Inch still supports numerous outdoor sports and an adjacent indoor sports centre is popular.

The Kings of Scotland had occasion to visit Perth when the Parliament met there and the **King James VI** Golf Club is named in honour of this ancient visitation of the golfing King. This club plays over a course laid out on the small sandy Moncrieffe Island in the middle of the River Tay. Its island position makes it unique among Scottish courses and it has to be reached by a rather exposed walk-way on the railway bridge over the Tay.

To the south of the town and perched above it is the **Craigie Hill** club, where good use of the contours of the land has been made. A remarkable view of Perth is obtained from the upper parts of the course. Outside of the town, there is a rich choice of golf at its best. There are the famous courses at **Gleneagles** (36), **Rosemount** (71), **Pitlochry** (66), and **Crieff** (14). In this area also are some delightful small courses—the six holes at **Glenshee** (1466 yds)—Scotland's smallest course, and the pleasurable 9 holes at **Killin** (43) **Comrie, St Fillans,** and **Strathtay** ('Members Dogs Only' says their notice).

Aberfeldy
Aberfoyle
Alyth (1)
Auchterarder
Blair Atholl
Blairgowrie (Rosemount) (71)
Callander (10)
Comrie
Craigie Hill, Perth
Crieff (14)
Dalmunzie, Glenshee
Dunblane
Dunkeld and Birnam
Dunning
Glenalmond

Gleneagles (36)
— King's Course
— Queen's Course
— Prince's Course
— Glendevon Course
Killin (43)
King James VI, Perth
Murrayshall, Perth
Muthill
North Inch, Perth
Pitlochry (66)
St. Fillans
Strathtay
Taymouth Castle, Kenmore

The North-East

Golf in the north-east of Scotland is of equal antiquity to that in the south. Since ancient times the game has been played at **Aberdeen** (3) and **Banff** (5) and probably also at the great links at **Peterhead** and **Fraserburgh** (30). Added to this is the continued success of the clubs round the coast, notably at **Cruden Bay** (15), **Buckie** (9), **Nairn** (60) and **Lossiemouth** (50). Further inland are the popular parkland courses such as **Elgin** (25), **Huntly** (41) and **Turriff** and the line of enjoyable courses on Deeside. A feature in this area is the number of open tournaments for all sorts of golfers, and a handicap player can easily construct a testing tournament circuit to toughen up their game in summer.

To the south of Aberdeen, beginning at **Stonehaven** (74), is another area rich in courses and golfing history. The major courses to choose from are at **Dundee** (18), **Carnoustie** (12), **Panmure** (64) and **Monifieth** (55).

Aboyne
Arbroath (Elliot)
Ashludie, Monifieth
Auchmill, Aberdeen
Auchinblae
Ballater (4)
Balgownie (3)
   (Royal Aberdeen)
Balnagask, Aberdeen
Banchory
Bon Accord,
   Aberdeen
Braemar
Brechin
Buckie (9) — Buckpool
          — Strathlene
Caird Park, Dundee
Caledonian, Aberdeen
Camperdown, Dundee

Carnoustie (12)
   — Burnside Course
   — Championship Course
Cruden Bay (15)
Cullen
Deeside, Aberdeen
Downfield, Dundee
Duff House Royal, Banff
Dufftown
Edzell
Elgin (25)
Forfar (27)
Forres
Fraserburgh (30)
Garmouth & Kingston,
   Fochabers
Hazlehead, Aberdeen
Hopeman
Huntly (41)

Insch
Inverallochy
Inverurie
Keith
Kemnay
King's Links, Aberdeen
Kintore
Kirriemuir
Lossiemouth (50) (Moray)
McDonald, Ellon
Monifieth (55)
Montrose (56)
  — Championship Course
  — Broomfield

Murcar (58)
Nairn (60)
Nairn Dunbar
Newburgh on Ythan
Old Meldrum
Panmure (64), Barry
Peterhead
Royal Tarlair, Macduff
Spey Bay
Stonehaven (74)
Tarland
Torphins
Turriff
West Hill, Aberdeen

The Highlands and Islands

The scarcity of golf courses in the west and north of this region is not the result of lack of suitable land: the west coast 'machair' and its maram grass, and the lusher turf in the Orkneys and Shetland Isles are immediately suitable for golf. But there has never been even one centre of population which could sustain the major courses that could so easily have been constructed. Instead there are a number of quiet, interesting, natural links courses.

Even so, some of the golfing sites here are of great antiquity. In Orkney, golf was recorded in 1585, and there are four courses now in the islands. The **Kirkwall** course is on moorland turf above the town, but the **Stromness** 18 holes are found in a more dramatic setting, close to the turbulent sea of the Hoy Sound where the Atlantic tides meet those of the North Sea. **Westray's** 9-hole course is the most inaccessible for the traveller in Scotland and serves both for golf and grazing. A minimum of two air journeys are required to reach it. Lastly, the oil terminal has meant that golf on **Flotta** is active again.

In Shetland, golf was formerly played at Sumburgh, on links shared with the air strip, and only two flights a day interrupted the golf. The discovery of oil banished golf from the now busy airport. Helped by donations from seven oil companies, a new course at **Dale** near Lerwick was built by the Shetland Golf Club. In the summer in these northerly isles, golf can be played at midnight.

In the Outer Hebrides the two courses are the parkland 18 holes at **Stornoway** and the links at **Askernish** in South Uist, where there is a sporty 9-hole course with a second set of tees used for the second time round. Green fees should be paid at the Lochboisdale Post Office two miles to the south.

On Mull, the view from the 9-hole **Tobermory** course is one of the best in Scotland with a long vista back down the Sound of Mull to the mountains of Lorne. The **Craignure** course is new, but **Colonsay's** course, abandoned in 1950, was reconstructed in 1979 from an old map. Professor Macneile Dixon's little course at

Iona has disappeared. **Tiree's** 9-holes are enjoyed by visitors as is the view from the links at **Sconser** in Skye which replaced the old Portree course. The **Machrie** course on Islay is rightly famous.

On the western mainland except for the clubs at **Oban** (63), **Spean Bridge** and **Fort William** (29), golf courses are few on the coast. The 9-hole courses at **Lochcarron** and **Traig** near Mallaig have a simple basic design which needs and gets little maintenance and there is a 9-hole course at **Gairloch,** the last on the west coast going north.

The north and east coasts are by contrast, well endowed with golf courses. **Reay** (69) and **Wick** (81) are notable in the north, and the choice of courses in the cluster at **Golspie** (37), **Brora, Dornoch** (17) and **Tain** (76) can hardly be bettered.

Further south **Inverness** (42) has a choice of courses, and in the Spey Valley there is an ample variety — **Grantown-on-Spey** (38), **Boat of Garten** (7), **Kingussie** (45) and **Newtonmore** (61).

Aviemore (Dalfaber) (2)
Alness
Askernish, South Uist
Boat of Garten (7)
Bonar Bridge
Brora
Carrbridge
Craignure, Mull
Colonsay
Dale (Lerwick), Shetland
Dornoch (Royal Dornoch) (17)
Flotta, Orkney
Fort Augustus (28)
Fort William (29)
Fortrose & Rosemarkie (70)
Gairloch
Golspie (37)
Grantown-on-Spey (38)
Helmsdale
Invergordon

Inverness (42)
Islay (Machrie) (52)
Lybster
Kingussie (45)
Kirkwall, Orkney
Lochcarron
Muir of Ord
Nethybridge (Abernethy)
Newtonmore (61)
Oban (63) (Glencruitten)
Reay (69)
Scalloway, Shetland
Sconser, Skye
Spean Bridge
Stornoway, Lewis
Strathpeffer Spa
Stromness, Orkney
Tain (76)
Tarbat, Portmahomack
Thurso

Tiree (Vaul)
Tobermory (Western Isles),
    Mull
Torvean, Inverness
Traigh, Mallaig
Westray, Orkney
Wick (81)

Index

Entries which are in italics have a detailed description in the book. The references are to page numbers.